ROUTLEDGE LIBRARY EDITIONS:
THE GERMAN ECONOMY

Volume 12

GERMAN ECONOMY, 1870–1940

GERMAN ECONOMY, 1870–1940
Issues and Trends

GUSTAV STOLPER

LONDON AND NEW YORK

First published in 1940 by George Allen & Unwin Ltd

This edition first published in 2018
by Routledge
2 Park Square, Milton Park, Abingdon, Oxon OX14 4RN

and by Routledge
711 Third Avenue, New York, NY 10017

Routledge is an imprint of the Taylor & Francis Group, an informa business

© 1940 Gustav Stolper

All rights reserved. No part of this book may be reprinted or reproduced or utilised in any form or by any electronic, mechanical, or other means, now known or hereafter invented, including photocopying and recording, or in any information storage or retrieval system, without permission in writing from the publishers.

Trademark notice: Product or corporate names may be trademarks or registered trademarks, and are used only for identification and explanation without intent to infringe.

British Library Cataloguing in Publication Data
A catalogue record for this book is available from the British Library

ISBN: 978-1-138-29360-1 (Set)
ISBN: 978-1-315-18656-6 (Set) (ebk)
ISBN: 978-0-415-78817-5 (Volume 12) (hbk)
ISBN: 978-1-315-22551-7 (Volume 12) (ebk)

Publisher's Note
The publisher has gone to great lengths to ensure the quality of this reprint but points out that some imperfections in the original copies may be apparent.

Disclaimer
The publisher has made every effort to trace copyright holders and would welcome correspondence from those they have been unable to trace.

GERMAN ECONOMY

1870–1940

Issues and Trends

BY

GUSTAV STOLPER

LONDON
GEORGE ALLEN & UNWIN LTD
40 MUSEUM STREET

FIRST PUBLISHED IN 1940
Copyright in the U.S.A.

PRINTED IN GREAT BRITAIN
KIMBLE & BRADFORD, LONDON, W.1

TO ALBERT PALACHE

THE TRUEST FRIEND AND MOST CRITICAL READER

PREFACE

THIS BOOK was completed a few days after Hitler's invasion of the Lowlands. In the months that have elapsed since then, the whole aspect of history has fundamentally changed. In the preface to the American edition I tried to appraise the effectiveness of the blockade as a decisive weapon in the life and death struggle between Western civilization and the Hitler revolution. I was never of the opinion that the blockade of Germany was as deadly a weapon against Hitler as a large sector of public opinion and some of the leading statesmen in Britain seemed to assume. It may by now have become evident that this war will be decided by military and political, not by economic means.

The following outline of the economic history of Germany covers the period from the founding of the Reich in 1870 to the outbreak of the Second World War in September 1939. It is an economic, not a political history that is told here. But in no nation's history are politics and economics so closely interrelated as in that of Germany. This indeed is the outstanding feature in the trend of German destinies. This book has not been written to defend a thesis. Yet it cannot help but reveal the very definite meaning of German history. The facts present their own comment and explanation. The

Preface

seventy years from the founding of the Bismarckian Reich to Hitler's nightmarish bid for world domination are interspersed with several catastrophes, including a world war, a democratic revolution, economic disaster through inflation, and the Nazi upheaval. The dramatic and tragic character of Germany's history in recent times is rarely borne in mind by those who look bewildered and puzzled at the German mystery.

This book reveals—I hope, clearly enough—three factors which should be brought to the awareness of the Western world. The first is the continuity in the underlying trends of German economic history. The Nazis hardly introduced a single element not preconceived or practised before. They could build on a foundation prepared for them by their predecessors. The totalitarian regime of the Nazis is merely the climax of the expansionist tendencies and responsibilities of governmental power over the destinies of the German people.

The second factor is the characteristic prevalence of "Statism" in German history ever since the days of Prussian ascendancy over the rest of Germany. Germany never passed through an age of individualism and liberalism. Individualistic tendencies were subdued in the 19th century by militarism, in the 20th century by collectivism. This explains why modern capitalism assumed other forms and entailed other effects in Germany than in the Western world.

viii

Preface

The third and last factor is the apparent failure of any mere economic interpretation and explanation of recent German developments. The phenomenon of Nazism cannot be understood on economic grounds. Despite the revolting corruption that enables the Nazi leaders to live in an imperial style, National Socialism as much as Bolshevism is essentially an ascetic philosophy, an ascetism, though, generated and nourished by envy and hatred, a very worldly ascetism aimed at power. I am afraid that this was never understood by Hitler's opponents, who clung to the naïve idea that National Socialism could be bought off by economic concessions. This mistake still lingers in many American minds which cannot conceive of a world driven by other motives than the quest for bigger and better profits and higher wages. But at last Great Britain seems to have begun to realize the true nature of the enemy she faces. If this unpretentious book can help to spread that understanding, it has served all its purpose.

The historian must not be a prophet. I therefore refrain from an attempt to appraise the future. It would be very tempting indeed to outline how far recent developments in Germany have strengthened or weakened her power of resistance in the new war. The new military technique of Germany, so surprising to the outside world, is a direct offspring of the military restrictions imposed on Germany after the last war. As Germany was denied general con-

ix

Preface

scription by the Versailles Treaty, she was induced to devise methods by which the tiny army of one hundred thousand professional soldiers might achieve its maximum effectiveness. The emphasis was therefore laid not on manœuvring masses, but on small units technically skilled to the limit and trained in independent action. Those are the men required for "Blitzkrieg" tactics, groups of fifty to five hundred men who by their skill and daring may decide a campaign.

The Germany economy was no less prepared for war than the military machine. German industry, too, had been trained for war for many years, under dire restrictions before Hitler, and free of restrictions since. This undoubtedly was the most important source of strength. All the problems of transition and adjustment from peacetime methods to wartime methods of production and distribution, technical and otherwise, that cause so much friction and delay to democratic nations with a free economy, did not exist for Germany. That country has been living on a war footing for several years. It was mobilized economically as well as militarily long before the war broke out. The two so-called Four Year Plans decreed by Hitler were nothing but war plans thought out and carried out to the minutest detail. Economic considerations were thoroughly subordinated to military requirements.

However, living on a war footing had heavily taxed the nerves as well as the material resources of

Preface

the German nation even before the supreme test of actual warfare started. Germany entered the war with a tired and unenthusiastic population and an industry operating at capacity limit with little possibility of further expansion. That will be felt ever more intensely the longer the war lasts. All the enthusiasm of the élite shock troops and all the perfection of the German war machine cannot compensate for that weakness unless the "Blitzkrieg" technique succeeds to the very end. On this technique Germany has staked her very existence. On the final success or failure of this technique the fate of our world depends. If this technique succeeds, not only are the British and French empires doomed. The face of the globe will be altered beyond recognition. The security of the Western hemisphere will be in imminent danger, its liberties and institutions exposed to attacks from without and disruption from within. Even with the utmost straining of our imaginations we shall hardly be able to cope with the realities.

Between to-day and the publication of this book Hitler may or may not have attempted to invade the British Isles. I have no doubt that such an attempt will fail. After Hitler's conquest of the European continent west of Russia, we had better adjust ourselves to thinking in terms of continents. If Hitler's Blitzkrieg fails, as we confidently expect it will, we must probably face an indefinite period of years during which the British Isles and the

Preface

European Continent will settle down—if settling it may be called—to a mutual siege. This siege once more will transform the face and fate of the world. It will not be just an episode after which the past may revive. The world thereafter will be very different from what it was before. If Germany has a few years in which to organize the continental life on her pattern, it will never be again the Europe we have known and loved. But at the same time, these next few years will affect just as deeply the continents outside Europe, and particularly their relationship to Great Britain.

This book has been written in the United States of America. I never believed that its publication would be much noticed, but so intensely is the American interest concentrated on Europe that America most eagerly tries to remedy her ignorance and to acquire knowledge of those "far away countries of which we know nothing," because she has suddenly grasped that America's own life may depend on timely understanding. Never before—probably not even in 1917–1918, when a large expeditionary force of Americans went to Europe to help to win the war—was America so conscious of her dependence on Europe's fate. In 1917 America went to war in order to defend what at that time she considered her rights, the freedom of the seas. If America enters this war, she will not do so in order to defend her rights, but to save her independence and her way of life. While Hitler

xii

Preface

may force his imprint on the enslaved Continent of Europe, a much larger event in the view of future historians will be the construction by the United States of America of the greatest military power the world has ever seen, placing her military establishments at the disposal of Great Britain and, at the same time, organizing twenty-one Latin American Republics in an effectively operating new League of American Nations. It is no longer Hitler's Germany against the Allies, it is Nazism against the combined Anglo-Saxon civilization and might. The greater part of the world is still open to the influence of Anglo-American civilization. This civilization, too, will undergo a fundamental transformation during the war. But it will be a transformation out of the spirit of its own past history, as Germany's future will be shaped by the ideas and forces of her history. We have to understand each great nation by its own history. Let us beware of simple, generalizing formulas.

*   *   *   *   *

For the preparation of this book I am greatly indebted to Dr. Alfred Braunthal, without whose help it might never have come into being. I wish gratefully to acknowledge his contribution. My thanks go also to Miss Martha Anderson for most competent editorial help.

G. S.

NEW YORK
August 1, 1940

CONTENTS

	PAGE
PREFACE	vii

PART I. INTRODUCTORY

PART II. TOWARD INDUSTRIAL WORLD POWER

1. Before the Unification of Germany	23
2. The Foundation of the Empire	26
THE FISCAL POWER OF THE FEDERAL STATES	29
THE UNIFICATION OF THE CURRENCY	31
THE FRUITS OF VICTORY	34
3. The Industrialization of Germany	36
THE GROWTH OF THE POPULATION	38
FROM AN AGRICULTURAL TO AN INDUSTRIAL NATION	40
4. The Importance of the Banks	44
THE INTERDEPENDENCE OF BANKING AND INDUSTRIAL CAPITAL	48
5. The Expansion of Foreign Trade	51
THE BANKS AS INSTRUMENTS OF FOREIGN TRADE AND CAPITAL EXPORT	53
GERMAN CAPITAL INVESTMENTS ABROAD	56
Drang nach dem Osten	58
6. From Liberalism to Protectionism	60
TOWARD A FREE-TRADE POLICY	62
THE TURN TO PROTECTIONISM	63

Contents

	PAGE
7. The Colonial Era	67
8. Government Ownership	70
THE NATIONALIZATION OF THE RAILROADS	71
HEAVY INDUSTRIES, PUBLIC UTILITIES, BANKS	75
9. Social Reform	77
10. The Organization of Business and Labor	83
THE CARTELIZATION OF INDUSTRY	83
THE FLOWERING OF TRADE-UNIONS	88
THE CO-OPERATIVES	91

PART III. THE WORLD WAR

1. War Finances	95
THE FINANCIAL MOBILIZATION	96
COSTS OF THE WORLD WAR	101
WAR LOANS AND BANK ADVANCES	103
WAR INFLATION	105
2. War Socialism	108
FEEDING THE NATION	111
COMPULSORY REGULATION OF INDUSTRY	116
3. Social Changes	120
THE WELFARE POLICY IN WARTIME	122
MEDIATION COMMISSIONS AND SHOP COMMITTEES	124
4. The End	125

PART IV. THE WEIMAR REPUBLIC

1. General Characterization	133
2. Inflation, 1918–1923	135
THE VERSAILLES TREATY	135
REPARATIONS	137

xvi

Contents

PAGE

2. Inflation, 1918–1923—*continued*

THE RUHR STRUGGLE · 142

FINANCIAL REFORMS · 145

THE WHIRL OF THE DEVISEN · 149

SOARING PRICES AND LAGGARD CIRCULATION · 152

INFLATION PROFITEERS · 157

INFLATION VICTIMS · 159

3. Stabilization · 162

THE "MIRACLE OF THE RENTENMARK" · 164

4. Plans for Reparation Payments · 168

THE DAWES PLAN · 168

THE YOUNG PLAN · 173

5. Prosperity · 176

6. Collapse · 181

THE AGRARIAN CRISIS · 182

THE BANKING CRISIS · 186

THE GERMAN MORATORIUM · 190

DEFLATION · 193

BRUENING'S EMERGENCY MEASURES · 196

7. Government and Business in Weimar Germany · 198

THE HERITAGE OF THE 1918 REVOLUTION · 198

THE SOCIALIZATION OF KEY INDUSTRIES · 200

HOUSING POLICY · 203

THE GOVERNMENT AS BANKER · 205

THE GOVERNMENT IN INDUSTRY · 208

LABOR POLICY · 210

MEDIATION AND ARBITRATION · 212

INDUSTRIAL DEMOCRACY · 216

PREPARED FOR HITLER · 218

8. Interlude · 220

xvii

Contents

PART V. THE THIRD REICH

	PAGE
1. The "Unalterable" Nazi Party Programme	229
ANTICAPITALISM	232
BREAKING THE BONDS OF INTEREST SLAVERY	235
THE NATIONALIZATION OF BIG INDUSTRY	239
2. Economic Policy	240
AGRICULTURE	243
INDUSTRY AND TRADE	246
METHODS OF FOREIGN TRADE	253
3. Financial Policy	255
FINANCIAL WINDFALLS	259
4. The Social Structure under National Socialism	264
5. Summary and Outlook	271
BIBLIOGRAPHY	277
INDEX	287

xviii

PART I

INTRODUCTORY

INTRODUCTORY

THIS BOOK covers a historical span of about seventy years, the Biblical life of man. In the first forty-three of these years, the German nation, united for the first time in its history, enjoyed unparalleled prosperity, political power, and economic expansion. In the following twenty-five years it had to go through five catastrophes equally unparalleled: 1914, 1918, 1923, 1933, 1939. And the next, most dreadful and possibly final, catastrophe already looms on the horizon—defeat in the present war, which may, once more, mean the end of a united Germany.

No other nation's history knows of such a sequence of rise and collapse. To the retrospective eye the years from 1870 to 1914 may appear as a unique episode. In almost two thousand years of European history there were German tribes and German states displaying various degrees of power and influence. But there never was a united Germany until 1871. German tribes overran the ancient Roman Empire and ruled over its dismembered parts. Emperors of the "Holy Roman Empire of the German Nation" were the masters of Europe in the Middle Ages. But not before 1871 was there a German nation that constituted an empire. In the centuries when England and France laid the foundations on which the

German Economy

structure of their unified states was built, the German people was split into hundreds of principalities and free cities, which fought and conquered one another according to the greater or lesser ambition and ability of their rulers. When in the sixteenth and seventeenth centuries the Reformation broke up the Catholic world, the religious wars of Europe were fought on German soil, by Germans against Germans, to the complete exhaustion of the physical substance of the German people and of its intellectual and economic life. Germany after the Thirty Years' war was a desert, depopulated and barbarized. Germany has never recovered from the effects of the Thirty Years' War. That war has shaped the character of the German nation, determined its history, molded its subsequent political and social evolution. As a political power Germany was wiped out after 1600. As an economic power that had flowered in the member towns of the Hanseatic League, and the wealthy commercial centers of western and southern Germany, it was annihilated. As an intellectual power, which after all had contributed Martin Luther and Albrecht Dürer to European civilization, it disappeared for almost a hundred years, in which, miraculously enough, Johann Sebastian Bach and Gottfried Wilhelm Leibnitz were born. Between 1640 and 1740—the century of flourishing power and civilization in England, France, and Spain—the European map seems to show a blank where later modern Germany was to arise.

4

Introductory

But the new Germany did not originate from this blank spot. What we understand as German history up to the seventeenth century has its scene of action almost entirely west of the Elbe and south of the Main. Here lay the rich flourishing towns where commerce and the arts thrived; here were the great monuments of German history, the cathedrals and monasteries and castles and proud mansions of wealthy patrician families; here the battles were fought, the peace treaties signed; here the German princes convened in their Reichstags; here the German kings were chosen by the electoral princes to receive the Holy Imperial Crown from the hands of the Pope in Rome.

From the end of the thirteenth century on, the rarely disputed leadership among the German princes was maintained by the Hapsburg dynasty. Originally a penurious Swiss family of knights risen to power in another period of chaos, such as seemed to be the ever recurring fate of that permanently amorphous part of Europe, the Hapsburgs acquired and expanded as family domain the southeastern corner of Germanic territory that much later became known as Austria, the poor Alpine provinces that gradually stretched from the Danube down to the Adriatic Sea. The Hapsburgs acquired but little land in Germany proper. Their imperialist drive was directed east, south, and west of German soil. They did not conquer their power, they married it. Even Charles V, the Hapsburg emperor who

German Economy

had to meet and to condemn Martin Luther and the Reformation, although German by blood (as far as the blood of any of the European dynasts can be ascertained), was a Spaniard by character and inclination. His residence was not in Vienna nor any other German town; it was Madrid, whence the Spanish expeditions were sent out over the oceans to open new worlds. The Austrian provinces and a few years before he died (1558) the German affairs, he left to his brothers and their descendants.

In 1526, the Hapsburgs, again by dint of a marriage contract, inherited the lands of the Bohemian and Hungarian crowns (or at least the disputed titles to them) when through the death in action of the last king the thrones of Bohemia and Hungary became vacant. By the middle of the sixteenth century the climax of Hapsburg influence had been reached. Except for Poland it covered about the area which four centuries later the Austrian Adolf Hitler proclaimed as German *Lebensraum* (living-space), including—by no means accidentally—Spain and Italy. But Germany proper, the country between the Rhine and the Elbe, between the North Sea and the Alps, lived her own life under her own princes, not much affected by the drives, successes, and failures of the Hapsburgs. The Thirty Years' War devastated the Hapsburg provinces as much as the western parts of the Reich. It is to be remembered that that war originated in Prague and Vienna. Its fury raged in Bo-

Introductory

hemia and Austria as much as in the Palatinate, in Saxony, Bavaria, and Swabia.

Only a few decades after the termination of this crucial war, at the end of the seventeenth century, a new Germanic power arose in the east—the Hohenzollern princes of the Mark of Brandenburg built up Prussia. The Hohenzollerns, like the Hapsburgs, came from the south, close to the Swiss border. But as early as 1415 a Hohenzollern was invested with the Mark of Brandenburg. When a century later (1525) the Hohenzollerns were made dukes of Prussia, they were under Polish overlordship. From then on, slowly but steadily and irresistibly, German history took its cue from the east. In 1640 the Great Elector Frederick William became Margrave of Brandenburg. He laid the foundation of the Prussian power. He defeated Poland with the help of the Swedes, and Sweden with the help of the Poles, and thereby acquired a country which in 1701 under his son, Frederick I was elevated to a kingdom.

From that time German history was dominated by the struggle for hegemony of two peripheral powers, Prussia and Austria. The huge majority of the peoples over whom the Hapsburgs ruled were, and remained to the very end, non-Germans. Only very late did Prussia become a German state. The great majority of the population of its eastern provinces undoubtedly was of Slavic origin, and a large part of the toiling classes spoke a Slavic dialect until late in the eighteenth century.

German Economy

Slavic tribes survived in the very neighborhood of Berlin up to our times, tenaciously preserving their language and their customs. Not until Frederick II (the Great), who ruled from 1740 to 1786, had conquered the Province of Silesia from the Austrian Empress Maria Theresa, did Prussia become predominantly German. Frederick II himself—today one of the canonized demigods of the Nazi interpretation of history—never spoke German, but French; he wrote his books in French and despised the German language as rude, barbarian, inarticulate. In fact, the great geniuses of German poetry, born in rapid succession from about the middle of the eighteenth century on, had to create their language from the poor remnants that survived the Thirty Years' War. But they again, without any exception, were not Prussians, nor were any of the radiant stars that arose on the sky of music, the great gift of the German race to mankind. Bach and Handel were Saxons, Mozart and Haydn Austrians, Beethoven a Rhinelander. The early history of Prussia has little to do with the arts and sciences. It is a history of statecraft, administrative efficiency, and military organization. It contributes a new and peculiar feature to the European picture: a new sort of state being built up by means of a new type of military organization and administrative machinery. The state is a creation by the dynasty, and the dynasty alone, out of a people uneducated, socially undifferentiated, only recently colonized and Christianized.

Introductory

From the very beginnings in Prussia the state was everything, not because of a preconceived philosophy, but because of the lack of creative forces other than the state, itself a creation of an ambitious dynasty and its military exploits. The state is the source from which both material and spiritual life emanate. Let us remember that the eighteenth century in which Prussia grew into a Great Power saw the birth of the capitalist system, the origins of modern industrialism with all its social consequences. In France, too, Louis XIV could proclaim the principle *"L'état, c'est moi!"* But the social stratification of the French people was variegated and complicated. It had its nobility, high and low, the hierarchy of the Catholic clergy, its bourgeoisie, its petite bourgeoisie, its peasantry, the beginnings of a pauperized proletariat. By the end of the eighteenth century, the "third" and "fourth" estates, together with the peasants, had overthrown the ruling feudal upper classes of nobility and clergy. The French Revolution was even preceded by the English revolution of a hundred and fifty years before. Prussia was free of social problems of that kind. In eighteenth-century Prussia there could be no class struggle, because there was only one class that mattered, the Junkers, who supplied the officers to the army and the civil servants to the administration. They were the state. Not before the conquest of Silesia did there exist in Prussia any substantial towns where a modern industry could evolve from ancient crafts. Industry

German Economy

in the Prussia of the eighteenth century was almost entirely a product of the Government. It was the Government that founded banks long before private banks were known. From the very beginning, the Government displayed all the initiative in the capitalist developments that in the Western world rested almost exclusively with private capitalists.

The historical fact of the omnipotence of the state dominated German philosophy; German philosophy did not create the omnipotent state. Fichte and Hegel had to deal with and to explain the accomplished reality. It was the world they lived in. It appeared as natural and familiar to them as the air they breathed. To the Prussian mind, the spiritual and social problems of the Western world hardly existed at the turn of the eighteenth and nineteenth centuries. The attack of the French Revolution was the attack of a national enemy. Napoleon was not the apostle of revolutionary ideas (as he appeared to many in western and southern Germany), but the tyrannical conqueror of the Prussian principles of law and order and discipline under a respected dynasty ruling by the grace of God.

With the defeat of Napoleon, Prussia established itself definitely in western Germany. From then on the fascinating process of Germany's becoming a self-conscious nation grew in scope and intensity. It was not Prussia that took the lead in this process of national emancipation and integration. Modern nationalism was

Introductory

a direct offspring of the French Revolution, and therefore suspect to all autocratic rulers, and particularly alien to Prussia. German nationalism in the first half of the nineteenth century was definitely liberal and democratic, and therefore was suppressed as dangerous to the existing order. In the abortive revolution of 1848 the later marriage of nineteenth-century nationalism and eighteenth-century Prussian absolutism was prepared. It was consummated after the victories of the Prussian armies—in 1864 over Denmark, in 1866 over Austria, and finally in 1871 over France. The prestige of Prussianism had reached its zenith. Prussian armies had realized the dream of the national unification that the liberals had longed for in vain since the days of Napoleon. The German Reich of Otto von Bismarck was the offspring of that marriage.

What happened after 1870 was the inevitable outgrowth of the peculiar origin of the new Reich. German liberalism, never deeply rooted in the masses even in western and southern Germany and virtually unknown outside of a tiny strata of intellectuals in East Elbian Prussia, had sold its soul to the principles of Prussian state power. This was the price for the achievement of national glory won by Prussia on the battlefields in France. What was left of independent thought, upright individualism, opposition against the deification of the state and the classes personifying the state, was crushed or corrupted by the ruthless genius of Bismarck.

German Economy

He broke the backbone of those classes which everywhere else were the most jealous of, and successful in preventing, encroachments of the governments upon the lives of the people.

Thus Germany acquired a strange cant that began to irritate and, increasingly, to terrify the world. Germany presented herself to the outside world as a great nation on the march to unlimited power and rapidly growing wealth, a nation successfully displaying all the resources dammed up by the adversities of centuries, a nation driven by genius and force that aroused the envy and the admiration of friend and foe. And yet, while the German leaders assured themselves loudly enough of steady and rapid progress in every direction, the country was not happy. There was something definitely unhealthy in the estrangement between the German Government, holding all the concentrated power of the most powerful state, and the intellectuals of the nation, who never really felt at home in the Bismarckian Reich. To be sure, we still speak of the nineteenth century as the era in which liberal principles held so strong a sway over the minds of Europe that even the autocratic leaders of half-absolutist governments felt constrained to render them their respect. Measured by Hitlerian standards, the Germany of Bismarck and William II was a free and liberal country. But measured by the standards of the Western world it was autocratic, authoritarian, unfree. The opposition was not arrested

Introductory

and sent to concentration camps, but it was subdued by more subtle means. The real power rested exclusively with the army and the bureaucracy, whose leading ranks were still recruited from, and dominated by, a few thousand Prussian Junker families. Whoever refused to sing their tune eliminated himself from any public career. They still were the state, and the state still refused to limit its power and pretensions.

It is futile to speculate about possibilities that might have existed had not the World War interfered. There are many good reasons to believe that Germany was on the road toward gradual democratization. The growing influence of the wealthy bourgeoisie, the intensified contacts with the world overseas, the definite change of the powerful Socialist party from a suspect revolutionary gang into a reliable mainstay of the existing order —all this and many other political and social forces tended toward a modernization of the whole setup of the state. Theobald von Bethmann-Hollweg, Reichs Chancellor after 1909, was a modern-minded man, a liberal conservative. The decisive issue then was the breakup of the stronghold of feudalism in the Prussian Diet. This diet still was elected on a franchise that secured its control by the landed aristocracy and its plutocratic allies. The other issue was a Reich government responsible to the parliament, not to the Emperor. But before these issues were settled the World War broke out.

German Economy

It is beyond the scope of this book to analyze the origins of the World War. Even today these origins are clouded by misconceptions spread by the war propaganda. The war originated not in Germany, but in Austria-Hungary. Whatever criminal blunders the Austrian statesmen might have committed, in the last resort the war became inevitable because the Hapsburg monarchy was a living negation of the two principal forces of the nineteenth and twentieth centuries: national and social emancipation. The shots of a fanatical, twenty-year-old Serbian student who assassinated the Austrian Archduke in Sarajevo, Bosnia, on June 28, 1914, were only the challenging signal that the existing order of Austria-Hungary had become untenable. This old Hapsburg monarchy, formed and expanded by dynastic marriages, was the giant stumbling-block to the aspirations for national unity of too many races. There were Poles, Ukrainians, Rumanians, Yugoslavs, Italians, who were ardent nationalists passionately desirous to join their racial brothers who lived outside of the monarchy. Only the Czechs lived altogether within the Austrian state, but they too were denied complete independence and even home rule. But any change of the status quo would have destroyed the precarious balance of the existing order.

Again we may wonder whether, over a period of time, the Dual Monarchy dominated by the German and Magyar elements might have been gradually trans-

Introductory

formed into a supranational federation, perhaps on the pattern of Switzerland. It just did not happen. Both Germany and Austria-Hungary were too rigid structures. They both failed to cope with the rising historical forces; they lacked the genius of constructive compromise that time and again made the survival of the British Empire possible. The pressure was too strong, so the explosion was inevitable. Austria-Hungary did not survive the war. The monarchy fell to pieces several months before it was broken up by the Paris peace treaties. When the statesmen of the Allied and Associated Powers met in Paris, the new succession states were already constituted in the area formerly ruled by the Hapsburgs. Nevertheless the order as established by the Allies created more problems than it settled.

In Germany the World War had revolutionary effects. It intensified and magnified to the extreme the underlying forces of German history. It made a nationalistic country even more nationalistic, a powerful government even more powerful. It merged the originally conflicting elements of German history into a new unit. By disrupting the continuity of life the war made a fundamentally conservative nation revolutionary. The old Prussia disappeared on August 4, 1914. This war soon turned out to be very different from the short glorious campaigns of 1864, 1866, and 1870, in the Bismarckian era. The whole nation, its entire man power and material resources, had to be mobilized and organ-

German Economy

·ized in order to resist the overwhelming pressure of a hostile world. The Socialist trade-unions, which up to this date were so to speak outside the pale of respectable society and the state it represented, became overnight distinguished instruments of the state machinery. Their official recognition implied their participation in political power. There were no constitutional changes during the war, but it seemed no longer doubtful that these changes were bound to come after the war. The Prussian state had a long-celebrated tradition of social-mindedness. It went back to the days of Frederick the Great ("The King is the first servant of the State"). It found its expression in the Social Security Laws passed under Bismarck, the earliest protective social legislation in any great nation, and exemplary for their time. It did not sound too far-fetched when Oswald Spengler, the famous author of *The Decline of the West,* published a pamphlet on Prussian Socialism which tried to prove the thesis that Prussianism and Socialism were essentially the same—one of many intellectual precursors of the subsequent National Socialism. The war broke down whatever limitations the nineteenth century had built around state power. There was nothing that was not subject to government regulation and covered by government responsibility. The German people accepted this condition with unquestioning readiness as a matter of course, not as a matter of principle.

The catastrophe of 1918-19 caught the German peo-

Introductory

ple unawares. They had been deluded and had indulged in self-delusion about the realities. It was a terrific awakening. In 1918 there was no revolution, there was a collapse. The Kaiser fled to Holland, the army was defeated and destroyed, the classes that had been responsible for German destiny for almost two centuries were annihilated or discredited. The defeat of 1918 left a vacuum. All real revolutions in history had been victories of ideologies preconceived and influential in the preparatory organization of the revolutionary forces. Nothing of that sort existed in Germany. When the army collapsed and revolution raised its head, there was one task only, to restore order and survive as a nation. Under the circumstances this was a superhuman task. Whatever the merits or demerits of the Versailles Treaty may have been, one fact should always be remembered: It created no peace. Large parts of German territory (among them some of the richest regions) remained occupied by foreign troops; important parts of the border in the west (Saar Region) and in the east (Upper Silesia) remained undefined; and above all, the grotesque reparation clauses made a restoration of orderly economic life utterly impossible. It is absurd to explain—as nationalistic and above all National Socialist propaganda did—all German postwar troubles by the Versailles Treaty alone, not by the effects of the lost war. However that may be, no German government would have been able to prevent the next catastrophe, 1923, which followed

German Economy

the French occupation of the Ruhr and the complete annihilation of the German currency through inflation. The first five years after the war reduced the authority of the German Government to a shadow, but they did not reduce the scope of necessary government interference and organization.

When by the end of 1923 the mark was stabilized, and in the spring of 1924 the Dawes Plan went into effect, a phenomenal recovery set in. The framework within which this prosperity was built up was not the result of a revolutionary ideology, for Germany remained a capitalist Republic by default of its anticapitalistic and antirepublican elements. It was a sort of directorate (in terms of the French Revolution), or a NEP (in terms of the Bolshevist Revolution), not too much spoiled by issues of principle.

The old ideologies had become meaningless and new ones had not appeared. Nobody had any program to offer. The Socialists were satisfied, the demands of their program having been completely realized up to the point from which they shrank themselves: the socialization of private industry. The Liberals had become conservative and the Conservatives were reactionaries. Once more, as in the days of William II, a general malaise spread over the German nation, which too easily begot disloyalty to the existing political order. As long as foreign troops stood on German soil and the Reparations Agent with his staff kept the Berlin government

Introductory

under tutelage, the stability of the regime was not threatened. It was a tragic coincidence that in 1930, together with the last French contingents and the Reparations Agent, prosperity disappeared from Germany.

The hurricane that blew from New York in the autumn of 1929 swept over Germany with deadly force. Once more Germany fell back into the restrictions of war economy. In 1931 the German banks were taken over by the Government; currency restrictions were reintroduced that were bound to result in a foreign-trade monopoly. Government orders were again the backbone of what was left of private business. In May, 1930, the republican constitution was irretrievably broken by Chancellor Heinrich Brüning in the misuse of the emergency paragraph of the Weimar Constitution. The Reichstag was dissolved, and the new elections in September, 1930, produced for the first time huge revolutionary parties, the National Socialists on the Right, and the Communists on the Left. From then on, step by step, the constitutional guarantees of civil liberties were eliminated. With diminishing authority the prerogatives usurped by the governments following each other in rapid succession were constantly increased.

On January 30, 1933, when Adolf Hitler was appointed Reichs Chancellor by a senile Reichs President who had never understood, and innumerable times had broken his solemn oath to uphold, the Weimar Constitution, there was in all Germany not a handful of men

German Economy

independent and willing to resist. The machinery of the state was finished to the last touch, holding in its grip every individual citizen in every walk of life. Hitler had only to press the button and the machine was made ready to work. His predecessors had done for him everything he needed. The trend toward Statism that pervaded the whole of German history after the resurrection of Germany under Prussian- leadership had reached its climax. The state owned the banks, the banks owned and controlled business, business controlled the jobs, and the masses who wanted the jobs had been trained by Marxist and anti-Marxist leaders alike to look to the Government for whatever they asked of life. The circle was closed. Hitler knew it. He promised the German people what it wanted, and they did not care about the means by which he fulfilled his promises. He kept these promises, except one—that he would preserve peace in making the German nation wealthy and dominant again. The Moloch state cannot stop, in Germany any more than in Russia or anywhere else. It devours its own children until it dies.

PART II

TOWARD INDUSTRIAL
WORLD POWER

TOWARD INDUSTRIAL
WORLD POWER

I. BEFORE THE UNIFICATION OF GERMANY

IT IS A COMMON BELIEF that Germany owes her rapid ascent to the position of the first industrial power of continental Europe to the founding of the Empire in 1871. On the whole this is true, but it would be a misconception to believe that before the Empire was founded Germany had been a poor agricultural country, far behind the countries of western Europe in industrial development. It is true that before 1870 the center of industrialization in Europe was west of the Rhine, and that only from there, primarily from England, did Germany derive the stimuli for her own industrialization. But when Bismarck forged the Reich with "blood and iron," "coal and iron" were already busy building up the economic foundations for this new Great Power.[1]

The chief advantage in industrialization a big nation enjoys over a smaller one is that it has a larger area free of tariff barriers and other trade impediments. Until the founding of the Reich the Germany of today was polit-

[1] In the *Economic Consequences of the Peace* (Macmillan & Co. Ltd.) J. M. Keynes says, "The German Empire was built more truly on coal and iron than on blood and iron" (p. 75).

23

German Economy

ically divided into about thirty states, only loosely connected. Before 1866 it was not even clear whether the Austrian monarchy with its whole territory—huge as compared with the various German states—would remain inside the German Bund and subsequently become the nucleus for the re-creation of a German Empire. But while politically this paramount question was still to be decided by the sword, economically the decision had been made more than a generation earlier.

The "smaller-Germany solution"—that is, the foundation of a German Empire under Prussian hegemony, excluding Austria—was enforced by Prussia in the victories on the Bohemian (1866) and French (1870-71) battlefields, but it had been perfected in the economic sphere as early as 1833. In this year Prussia succeeded in uniting the most important of the future German federal states in the framework of the German Zollverein. Other states joined rapidly, and after 1854 the Zollverein encompassed all the territory that in 1871 was to be included in the German Reich except Mecklenburg, Hamburg, Bremen, and the territories annexed in the subsequent wars (Schleswig-Holstein and Alsace-Lorraine).

The German Zollverein represented a complete customs union. Traffic among the member states was not impeded by any kind of customs barriers. The only customs frontiers were those between the member states and the world outside, to which, in this respect, Austria

Toward Industrial World Power

belonged. This, however, was as far as German unification went at that time. There was neither a common currency nor even freedom of movement and of settlement among the member states. Nevertheless, the Zollverein proved to be a potent stimulant for economic development. Many authors even see in it the chief reason for the economic flowering of Germany in the period before the founding of the Reich, although foreign factors contributed. Some of these were: the agrarian reforms of the Napoleonic Era; the influences from the French domination over western Germany; and the influx of British capital and British enterprise. In any event, in the 1840's German economy began to reveal its driving power.

In several German districts simultaneously modern industry began to develop—primarily in those areas where various kinds of local and home trades had for some time been prosperous. Agriculture, hitherto dominant in German economic life, underwent a process of modernization and intensification. The first modern credit banks appeared, and Germany's first promoters' boom occurred between 1848 and 1857, when the discovery of the Californian gold fields gave the most powerful stimulus to the entire American-European world. For Germany this was the period of the first rapid development of railroads, banking, and heavy industries. This promoters' boom ended in the international crisis of 1857.

German Economy

Thus, on the eve of the founding of the Empire, Germany was still what according to present-day yardsticks would be called an agricultural country. In 1871, of a population of 41,000,000, 64 per cent lived in the country (that is, in communities with fewer than 2,000 inhabitants). Measured by the standards of that time, however, German industry shows not inconsiderable achievements. Thus in 1871, 29,400,000 tons of coal and 8,500,000 tons of lignite were mined in Germany, including Luxembourg. The output of iron ore was 4,400,-000 tons, the production of pig iron, 1,564,000 tons, in contrast to a British annual production of from 6,000,000 to 7,000,000. Among other industries that of textiles was relatively highly developed in some parts of the country, whereas machine and chemical industries were still in their infancy. Several substantial enterprises were already in existence in the machine industry, such as that of Krupp in Essen, which as long ago as 1873 employed 16,000 persons, and that of Borsig in Berlin. To what a high level Germany had advanced economically may be gauged from the fact that in 1870 the railroad system had a mileage of 18,650 kilometers (11,501 miles). The United States had 52,922 miles.

2. THE FOUNDATION OF THE EMPIRE

When Austria and the German states allied with her were finally defeated in the short war of 1866, and after

Toward Industrial World Power

the North German states had been united by Prussia to form the North German Federation (Nord-Deutscher Bund), the foundation of the "Smaller German Reich" under Prussian leadership could be a question of but a few years. It is a relevant historical fact, however, that five years later, after another victorious campaign, the Reich was founded in the heart of the conquered enemy country, France. Thus the economic effects of the unification and of the victory over a prosperous country coincided and enhanced one another.

The customs union had prepared the ground, and the German nation derived immense additional economic advantages from its newly gained political unity. First of all, the unification of economic legislation was extremely beneficial. Business needs had already enforced unification in some specific fields of commercial law. In 1847 the first draft of a Common German Bills-of-Exchange Law (Allgemeine Deutsche Wechselordnung) had been completed, and during the following four years it was enacted in the various member states of the Zollverein. In 1861 the draft of a Common German Commercial Code was completed; by 1865 it had been ratified by almost all the German states, including Austria. Nevertheless, essential conditions of economic activity remained different in different states.

Not until the Reich was founded could trade regulations for the whole territory be unified. Conditions for

German Economy

the exercise of all trades that had hitherto been restricted were now regulated in the spirit of liberalism then predominant in Germany. Thus for the first time complete freedom of movement for individuals and merchandise inside the Reich's territory was secured. In the same way, measures and weights, until then varying widely in the different states, were unified on the basis of the metric system. The post office became a Reich enterprise, except in Bavaria and Württemberg, which lost their "postal sovereignty" only when the Reich was remodeled in the 1918 revolution.

But the "postal sovereignty" of the chief South German states was not the only, nor the most important, relic from the time of division into many petty sovereignties, which lasted up to the end of the nineteenth century. Common law prevailed within the domain of the federal states, the Reich Civil Code not being enacted until the beginning of the twentieth century. Even after the railways had been nationalized they remained the property of the various major states (Prussia, Bavaria, Saxony, Baden, Württemberg) until transferred to the Reich by the reforms after the World War. And, most important of all, the individual states virtually retained financial sovereignty, apart from a few reservations vested in the Reich.

Toward Industrial World Power

THE FISCAL POWER OF THE FEDERAL STATES

Like the United States of America, the German Reich began as a federation of sovereign states, and it retained this status until the revolution of 1918. But while, as far as foreign and even domestic politics were concerned, Germany quickly became a unified state, the financial and administrative power remained chiefly with the individual states up to the time of the Weimar Constitution.

The Reich had no administrative organs except the army, the navy, the foreign service, the customs administration, the post office, and, later, the colonial administration. The entire internal administration—police, judiciary, fiscal administration, and schools—remained in the hands of the federal states. Accordingly, the Reich had little freedom of action in the field of fiscal policies. From the Zollverein period the Reich was in control of the customs revenues and of some excise taxes, which, however, were rather narrow in scope before the World War. Older even than the customs revenues was another peculiar kind of Reich revenue, the so-called matricular contributions. Originally, these were the payments the member states of the German Bund, formed in 1815 after Napoleon's collapse, made to the Bund to keep up its rather shadowy existence. The North German Federation and Bismarck's Reich inherited this revenue. In a way the

German Economy

Reich thus remained dependent on the federal states. After 1880, when the federal states were awarded a share of certain indirect Reich taxes, this was, however, true merely in form. The matricular contributions paid by the states to the Reich and the transfers from the Reich to the states out of indirect taxation approximately balanced.

The only important new source of revenue the North German Federation and Bismarck's Reich exploited for themselves was the revenue from the post office and the telegraph, to which in 1871 was added the income from the management of the Alsace-Lorraine railroads. It is therefore not surprising that up to 1913, the eve of the World War, the ordinary and extraordinary revenue of the Reich, 4,121,000,000 marks, was exceeded by the Prussian revenue of 4,241,000,000 marks, to which must be added the revenue of the other federal states, amounting to 2,476,000,000 marks. The Reich debt, 4,897,-000,000 marks as of October 1, 1913, was considerably below the Prussian debt, 9,902,000,000 marks, and the debt of the other federal states, 6,295,000,000 marks (figures for most of the states as of April 1, 1913). It should be noted, however, that the states' debts included the railway bonds.

Before the Weimar Constitution, the whole field of direct taxation was a prerogative of the federal states (which derived considerable revenue also from the railroads), while the chief income of the municipalities was

Toward Industrial World Power

derived from real-estate taxation. In addition, the municipalities raised surtaxes on the state income taxes.

Not before the last years preceding the World War could the Reich penetrate to some extent into the field of direct taxation. In 1906 it was allotted a share in the estate taxes, which until then had been purely state taxes. Their administration, however, remained with the states, and returns from them were always very small. The first more incisive inroad into the traditional tax system occurred under the shadow of the impending World War. In 1913 the Reich imposed a capital levy for the special purpose of financing armament. The purpose was expressed in its name: defense contribution (*Wehrbeitrag*). Its revenue, which reached the Treasury in 1914 and 1915, amounted to approximately 1,000,000,-000 marks.

Thus, economically, the Reich was set up in three stages: the first was the creation of the Zollverein in 1833; the second, the political formation of the Reich in 1871; the third, the revolution of 1918. There is no doubt that of these stages that of 1871 was by far the most important.

THE UNIFICATION OF THE CURRENCY

At the time of the founding of the Reich, Germany was still divided into seven separate currency areas. Furthermore, there were thirty-three banks of issue entirely

German Economy

unconnected with one another and carrying on their issuing activities under completely different rules and laws.

With such a chaotic currency system, any monetary policy in an industrialized country would have been impossible. The one feature common to all these currencies—except that of Bremen, where the legal tender was gold—was that silver was legal tender. The states had certain agreements with one another as to the relative value of their respective currencies. Gold coins also circulated in all German states, their ratios to the legal silver currency fluctuating except in Prussia, where the ratio between gold and silver money was fixed by law.

The unified currency of the new Reich was based on the gold standard. The adoption of the gold standard was of extraordinary significance at a time when no great country besides Great Britain had yet introduced it. But when Germany reached this momentous decision, the great crisis of silver was already in the offing, and it was to be expected that France and the United States would also soon conform to the gold standard. By taking the lead the young German Reich rendered a great service to world economy. It cleared the path to an international currency unification on the gold basis, which for the whole period up to the World War proved of the greatest importance for the rapid expansion of world trade. The individual to whom the credit belongs primarily is the liberal politician and economic

Toward Industrial World Power

theorist Ludwig Bamberger. Of course, some credit is due Bismarck himself and his Secretary of State, Rudolf von Delbrück, who until his resignation in 1876 had a strongly liberal influence on the new German economic policy. For Germany herself the adoption of the gold standard reflected the liberal "Western orientation" predominant in the Germany of the earlier Bismarck and at that time characteristic of his personal attitude.

The new currency system was introduced in three stages. 1. In 1871 a law concerning the minting of gold coins was passed. The mark was adopted as the new currency unit, its ratio to the value of the current silver coins was defined, and the latter were withdrawn. 2. In 1873 the gold standard was established by law, and silver was limited to small coin. 3. In 1875 one of the thirty-three central banks, the Prussian Bank, was transformed into the Reichsbank. The other banks of issue were thereby forced into a very precarious position, in relation to both the Reichsbank and the commercial banks. The object was to induce them to give up voluntarily to the Reichsbank the fixed contingents of banknotes still reserved for them by law. By 1910, in fact, twenty-seven of the issuing banks had yielded to this pressure; the rights of issue of the other five banks were not canceled until 1935. The note circulation of these "private issuing banks," as these institutions were called after the creation of the Reichsbank, was however so small and so strictly regulated that it was

German Economy

scarcely a disturbing feature in the new monetary policy.

The unification of the Reich was of undoubted and permanent benefit to the German industrial system. The benefits accruing from the victory over France were rather doubtful, and certainly not permanent.

THE FRUITS OF VICTORY

The annexation of Alsace and Lorraine, two of the most prosperous French provinces, unquestionably became a source of wealth for one and a half German generations. The textile industry was the most highly developed among the local industries (except agriculture). In the new Reichsland (Reich Dominion) were more than half as many cotton spindles as in the rest of Germany, and almost as many mechanical looms. Germany was thus chiefly indebted to the new provinces for the growing prosperity of her textile industries.

The abundant wealth of Alsace-Lorraine in minerals, on the contrary, was almost untapped. Only after the process of iron-ore treatment invented by the Englishmen Thomas and Gilchrist had been introduced into Germany (in 1879) could the rich ore mines of Lorraine be exploited. The German steel industry was then expanded on this basis, and it became one of the main factors in the rapid progress of Germany's industrial power. The iron-ore deposits of Lorraine are estimated

Toward Industrial World Power

at 700,000,000 tons of metallic iron as against only 300,-000,000 tons in postwar Germany.

At the beginning of the twentieth century another treasure was found—the Alsacian potash mines. Together with the central German deposits they gave Germany a virtual monopoly on the potash markets of the world. When Alsace-Lorraine was ceded to France by the Versailles Treaty, Germany lost both the ore basis for her steel industry and half of her potash world monopoly.[2]

The French war indemnity imposed in 1871, however, did not prove an unmitigated blessing for Germany. It is often asserted that to this contribution of 5,000,000,000 gold francs Germany owed the secure foundation of her gold currency. It is true, Germany was able to use the 273,000,000 francs that France paid in gold to build up a gold reserve, and her balance of payments profited by the influx of the French billions. It is also true that the sudden influx of foreign billions started a tremendous boom in German business that went far beyond what would have happened normally because of the enthusiasm over the formation of the Reich. It is easy to imagine the change it must have meant to the very narrow German security market that

[2] A few years after the World War the German and French potash interests were pooled for the common exploitation of foreign markets. Meanwhile, however, this monopoly was largely destroyed by the discovery and development of potash deposits in other countries, such as the United States, Poland, and Palestine.

German Economy

a major part of the debt of the German federal states could be repaid within a short period out of the proceeds of the war indemnity. The result was a promoters' boom of unprecedented intensity and extent.

In 1870 the capital of all Prussian joint-stock companies (with limited and unlimited liability) taken together amounted to 3,078,000,000 marks. By 1874, 857 new companies with a capital of 3,307,000,000 marks had been added. The speculative frenzy gained particular impetus in railroads and heavy industries.

Perhaps in some ways German industries were permanently benefited by this boom. But, aided and abetted by the freedom from any restraining regulations so characteristic of that era, a great many of the enterprises starting up at that time were of an incredibly reckless and fraudulent nature. The result was the crash of 1873-74, as unprecedented in its dimensions as the preceding boom. Of 857 companies founded in the "building years," in December, 1874, as many as 123 were in liquidation and 37 were in bankruptcy.

The years 1873-74 were sad for all the industrial countries of the world, and they marked only the beginning of a long-drawn-out period of depression.

3. THE INDUSTRIALIZATION OF GERMANY

On the eve of the founding of the Reich, Germany's economic character was predominantly agricultural, but

Toward Industrial World Power

the process of industrialization had already begun. The impulses derived from the foundation of the Empire, however, were of the greatest importance for Germany's industrial development, and in a few years carried her to the first rank of the industrial countries of Europe. This should not be mistaken to imply that Germany—after the example of Great Britain—sacrificed her agriculture to her industrial expansion. As will be more extensively shown below, the German Government came to the aid of agriculture by means of a tariff—at the price of raising the cost of living for the industrial population—as soon as the threat of American competition began to be felt on the grain market, the broad basis of German agriculture. In fact, German agriculture continued its spectacular expansion, mainly through the progress of agricultural technique. German grain and potato production approximately doubled between the foundation of the Reich and the World War, partly thanks to increased acreage, but mainly because of improved yield per unit under cultivation. If we compare the yields of 1878 and 1879 with the average of 1901-10, the average per hectare (2,471 acres) rose for wheat from 1.35 to 1.96 metric tons; for rye, from 1.06 to 1.63; for potatoes, from 7.11 to 13.51.

German Economy

THE GROWTH OF THE POPULATION

Nevertheless, German agriculture was no longer able to satisfy the food requirements of the German population. From being a grain-exporter Germany was consequently gradually transformed into an importing country. The population increase was so gigantic and the food standards of the people improved so decidedly that even the doubling of the grain production was insufficient to feed them all. The growth in population that followed industrialization, and in its turn furnished the basis for further industrialization, continued without a break up to the World War.

TABLE I

Population on Reich Territory

	Population	Increase by decades
1816	24,833,000	
1825	28,113,000	13.2%
1835	30,802,000	9.6
1845	34,290,000	11.3
1855	36,138,000	5.4
1865	39,548,000	9.4
1875	42,518,000	7.5
1885	46,707,000	9.9
1895	52,001,000	11.3
1905	60,314,000	16.0
1915	67,883,000	12.5

The natural increase in the German population was actually even greater than shown by Table 1. Part of

Toward Industrial World Power

this increase was offset by emigration, which between the 1840's and the 1880's became a mighty stream. Not before the end of the 1880's had German national wealth increased sufficiently and German industry developed such a demand for labor that the economic motive for emigration practically disappeared. Between 1840 and the World War 5,000,000 Germans emigrated overseas. After 1890 emigration petered out, as is shown by Table 2.

TABLE 2

Overseas Emigration from Germany

1821–30	8,500
1831–40	167,700
1841–50	469,300
1851–60	1,075,000
1861–70	832,700
1871–80	626,000
1881–90	1,342,400
1891–1900	529,900
1901–10	279,600
1911–20	91,000
1921–30	567,300
Total	5,989,400

After the beginning of the nineteenth century, the country of destination was almost exclusively the United States. Of the 5,989,400 Germans who emigrated overseas between 1820 and 1930, 5,329,400 went to the United States.

The emigration to overseas countries was partly off-

German Economy

set by continental immigration, chiefly from Austria-Hungary, Italy, and the western parts of Russia (especially Poland). This immigration increased steadily until in the last two decades before the World War it exceeded emigration. Germany had become—on balance—an underpopulated country.

FROM AN AGRICULTURAL TO AN INDUSTRIAL NATION

Despite the intensification of agriculture, the rural sector participated to only a negligible degree in the growth of the population. As in other industrial countries, rural life lost its attractions. A flight from the land began, with the result that the natural increase in population was absorbed by the cities, whither people were attracted by the growing demand for labor at rising wages and by the amenities of urban life. Table 3, which summarizes the census, beginning with the first in 1882, shows this shift.

The trend from 1871 to 1882, for which a detailed census is not available, was not difficult. Thus the remarkable fact appears that since the foundation of the Reich agriculture and industry had about exchanged their relative importance in Germany's economic life.

The broad foundation for Germany's industrial expansion was created by the development of her heavy industries. In coal-mining Germany never caught up with her rival, Great Britain, but even so, German coal-

Toward Industrial World Power

mining expanded at a rate with which only that of the United States is comparable. Hard-coal production rose from an annual average of 34,500,000 tons in the period 1871-75 to 191,500,000 in 1913. The rich bituminous mines were increasingly developed, and the production of bituminous coal increased from 9,700,000 tons to 87,500,000 tons in the same period.

TABLE 3

Number of Gainfully Employed

	1882	1907	1925	1933
	(three ciphers omitted)			
Agriculture and forestry ...	7,135	8,557	9,763	9,343
Industry and crafts	5,988	9,981	13,479	13,053
Commerce and communications	1,420	3,441	5,185	5,939
Public and private services ..	984	1,712	2,188	2,699
Domestic service	1,358	1,465	1,394	1,296
Total	16,885	25,156	32,009	32,296

Percentage of Total

	1882	1907	1925	1933
Agriculture and forestry	42.3	34.0	30.5	28.9
Industry and crafts	35.5	39.7	42.1	40.4
Commerce and communications .	8.4	13.7	16.2	18.4
Public and private services	5.8	6.8	6.8	8.4
Domestic service	8.0	5.8	4.4	3.9
	100.0	100.0	100.0	100.0

The German iron industry owed its expansion as much to its coal basis as to the ore mines of Lorraine.

German Economy

German iron-ore production increased from an annual average of 5,300,000 tons in the period 1871-75 to 28,-700,000 tons in 1913. This provided the foundation for the growth of the iron industry. In 1871 German pig-iron production was 1,564,000 tons; in 1910, 14,794,000 tons of pig iron (Luxembourg always included). As late as 1900 British pig-iron production (9,103,000 tons) exceeded the German-Luxembourg production (8,521,-000 tons), but in steel Germany (7,372,000 tons) already beat her British rival (5,981,000 tons). In 1910 German iron production was far ahead of all other European countries; Great Britain with 10,172,000 tons of pig iron and 7,613,000 tons of crude steel had been left far behind.

Germany made use of her heavy industries (1) to build up her railroad system (her railroad mileage increased from 18,560 kilometers in 1870 to 60,521 kilometers in 1912); (2) to create one of the mightiest merchant fleets in the world (her mercantile steamer fleet increased from 147 ships with 81,994 gross register tons in 1871 to 2,098 ships with 4,380,348 gross register tons in 1913); (3) to expand her machinery industry at a gigantic pace into one of the largest sources of exports (51,000 workers were employed in 1861, 356,000 in 1882, and 1,120,000 in 1907). Finally, the position taken by the armament industries should not be overlooked. In 1912 the firm of Krupp of Essen employed 68,300 workers.

Toward Industrial World Power

But the special pride of Germany at this time was her electrotechnical and chemical industries. In absolute size, as measured by the number of employees, both were far smaller than other industries. But their importance for German industrialization, foreign trade, and prestige was enormous.

The progress of the electrical industries is tied up with the names of Werner von Siemens and Emil Rathenau, the father of Walter Rathenau, later Foreign Minister of the Republic, who in 1921 fell a victim to nationalistic fanatics. Siemens was an ingenious inventor who as early as 1867 constructed a dynamo, and in 1879 studied the problem of electrical railroad traction. He became the founder of the Siemens concern, which together with the A.E.G. (German General Electric Company) completely dominates the German electrical industry. With the firm of Siemens, Emil Rathenau founded in 1883 the German Edison Company for Applied Electricity, which, under Rathenau's leadership, soon broke loose from Siemens and formed the company that later became the A.E.G. To both these groups must be ascribed the electrification of Germany, the construction of her extensive trolley systems and of municipal and overland power-transmission systems, and the development of high- and low-voltage techniques in general.

The chemical industry did not have to start from

German Economy

scratch as did the electrical industry. Some tradition had already accumulated. Justus von Liebig's importance for agricultural chemistry may be recalled. But in the chemical industry also the decisive expansion occurred during the five decades of the Empire. The great chemical concerns, later amalgamated in the I.G. German Dye Works, date from then. After this amalgamation the company dominated the German chemical industry in an almost monopolistic way. The world-wide fame of the German dye industry was established during this period, as was that of German pharmaceutical chemistry, and of many other chemical products.

4. THE IMPORTANCE OF THE BANKS

No account of German industrialization would be complete without giving full consideration to the leading role of the German banks. The dynamics of German economy can be understood only if one realizes that—in contrast to America and England—one of the most powerful stimuli to industrialization came from the peculiar banking system of Germany. The great difference between the German and Anglo-Saxon banking systems becomes apparent in the difference in meaning of "bank" in Germany and in England and America. The German bank is a combination of commercial bank, investment bank, and investment trust, a combination which—as will be shown more in detail—cannot

Toward Industrial World Power

conceivably work otherwise than by the backing of a central bank.

Until the World War merely a minor part of the funds of a typical German bank were invested in government securities—long-term bonds and Treasury bills. Another part was invested in commercial bills, which could be rediscounted with the Reichsbank and therefore could be used as a liquid reserve. But the funds were used chiefly for direct, and mostly long-term, loans to industrial and commercial enterprises—whether secured or unsecured—and for industrial promotions. Industrial promotions or capital issues were either made by one bank alone or, if larger enterprises were involved, by a group of banks, so-called consortiums or syndicates. The bank or the group of banks would take over the stocks or bonds to be issued at a fixed price and then try to place them with the public. In consequence, the banks had substantial holdings of stocks and bonds of industrial and commercial companies permanently in their portfolios. In addition they purchased stocks and bonds either in order to regulate market values or for pure speculation.

To be able to shoulder the risks connected with these transactions the banks needed a large capital. As a rule, capital, reserves, and surplus of German banks amounted to about 25 per cent of their deposits and other liabilities. When, much later, through the World War and

German Economy

the subsequent inflation, the capital of the banks melted away, the banking crisis became inevitable. The banks derived their deposits largely from the enterprises they financed, while the savings of the public at large went mainly into savings banks (mostly municipal).

From the very moment of their foundation the German banks were planned mainly as instruments for the financing of industries, not as credit banks after the English and American pattern. According to Schulze-Gävernitz the banks were founded in the 1840's in a revolutionary spirit as instruments of the industries for financing their enterprises in opposition to the private bankers as representatives of *"haute finance."* [3] They were at that time the almighty masters of the capital market, culminating in the House of Rothschild, formerly of Frankfort-on-Main but now international in scope. It was not by mere chance that the first German bank, the A. Schaaffhausensche Bankverein in Cologne, was founded in the year of revolution, 1848. The first constitutional Cabinet in Prussia provided this institution with its charter, which included the privilege of issuing banknotes.

How revolutionary these ideas on financing industries seemed in those days becomes evident when we remember that it was the time of Proudhon's schemes, which left their characteristic imprint on the French Crédit Mobilier. Following these same principles, Gustav von

[3] G. von Schulze-Gävernitz, *Die deutschen Kreditbanken, 1922,* p. 31.

Toward Industrial World Power

Mevissen, the originator of the Schaaffhausensche Bank-verein, made the promotion of industries the chief concern of this first German bank. This bank was responsible for the formation in 1849 of the first stock company in the German mining industry, the Kölner Bergwerksverein, also of the first steel plant and of the first machine factory, as stock companies.

In view of this close interrelation between the origins of banking and industry in Germany it is only natural that the two important industrial boom periods before the World War—the early 1850's and the early 1870's—coincided with the formation of the great banks. In both these periods a relatively large part of the available promoters' capital went into new banks. Almost all the large German banks originated during these two periods. The Schaaffhausensche Bankverein was followed by the Disconto-Gesellschaft in 1851, which in 1856 was developed into a regular bank; furthermore, by the Darmstädter Bank in 1853 and the Berliner Handels-gesellschaft in 1856. In the second period, the Deutsche Bank was founded in 1870 and the Dresdner Bank in 1872.

German Economy

THE INTERDEPENDENCE OF BANKING AND INDUSTRIAL CAPITAL

Until today the German banks have in essentials remained true to their original pattern. This should not, however, be taken to imply that all industries have been founded by them and are still under their control. Very frequently, perhaps even in the majority of cases, the initiative lay not with the banks but with individual industrial promoters. The importance of the contribution of the banks in the initial period, and accordingly of their permanent influence, varies widely with the individual industries and enterprises. But in one way or another the banks had their hand in almost all promoting and developing activities, and remained financially interested in the industries concerned.

The permanent influence of the banks on industry was much enhanced by the voting practice: Their voting power in the stockholders' meetings was derived not only from their own holdings of the stock of these industrial companies but in addition from those of their customers. Possessed of this voting power and relying on their influence as underwriters, the banks participated directly in the management of industries, delegating their own officers to the boards of directors of their industrial corporations. Conversely, the large industrial concerns were represented on the boards of the banks with which they had business connections.

Toward Industrial World Power

In the heavy industries the largest enterprises, such as Krupp's and Thyssen's, were originally independent, but gradually even their relations to the banks became closer, and the large banks started a keen competition among themselves for making intimate contacts with the heavy industries. In the end every one of the big banks had its connections with some leading heavy industrial groups.

The close relation between banks and industries was instrumental in fostering the concentration in both fields. In the course of its rapid growth industry shifted its weight more and more from the smaller and middle-sized companies to those concerns which from their beginnings demanded huge capital investments for their management, such as the heavy industries, the electrical industries, and shipbuilding. In this process it became increasingly necessary for large, efficient, and rich banks to be ready to shoulder the task of financing. Thus industrial concentration became a powerful incentive for the concentration of banking.

The Berlin banks spread over the provinces by forming branch institutions and by amalgamating smaller, and later even large, provincial banks. Thus the Deutsche Bank in 1897 took over the Hannoversche Bank, and in 1903 the Essener Creditanstalt, both powerful banks closely connected with flourishing industries. In 1895 the Disconto-Gesellschaft took over the Norddeutsche Bank.

German Economy

At the end of this process even the large banks began to amalgamate among themselves. The prewar era witnessed only one of these amalgamations. In 1914, just preceding the outbreak of the war, the Schaaffhausensche Bankverein was taken over by the Disconto-Gesellschaft. After the war this process of concentration was resumed with growing impetus. The most important features were the amalgamations of the Mitteldeutsche Privatbank with the Commerz- und Discontbank under the firm name Commerz- und Privatbank in 1920; the amalgamation of the Darmstädter Bank with the Nationalbank für Deutschland under the name of Darmstädter und Nationalbank in 1921. Finally the last phase—characterized by the amalgamation of the Deutsche Bank and the Disconto-Gesellschaft in 1929 and by the taking over of the Darmstädter Bank by the Dresdner Bank following the banking crash of 1931—resulted in a practical monopoly of less than half a dozen banks.

The following figures show how far the concentration in German banking had already advanced before the war: At the end of 1910, 48.3 per cent of the deposits of all the commercial banks with at least 1,000,000 marks share capital were held by the large Berlin banks (including the Darmstädter Bank and the Schaaffhausensche Bankverein); and of these 40.2 per cent were held by the four so-called D-Banks alone

50

Toward Industrial World Power

(Deutsche Bank, Disconto-Gesellschaft, Dresdner Bank, and Darmstädter Bank). In 1911 the capital (share capital plus reserves) of all the commercial banks with at least 1,000,000 marks share capital amounted to 3,731,000,000 marks; of this total 2,721,000,000 marks were represented by the four D-Banks and the Schaaffhausensche Bankverein, including the banks affiliated with them.[4]

On the other hand, the concentration among the banks accelerated the concentration in industry. After banking concentration had progressed to some extent it happened more and more frequently that the big banks took up an interest in several industries that worked in the same line, or in other branches of industry whose production was technically interconnected. This again favored a monopolistic trend. The banks used their influence over the industries to bring about horizontal or vertical combinations or cartels.

5. THE EXPANSION OF FOREIGN TRADE

Another fundamental feature of the German banks before the World War was the leading role they played in the economic and political expansion of Germany outside her own frontiers. It should be noted that the expansion of her industries had raised Germany to the

---

[4] According to J. Riesser, *The German Great Banks and Their Concentration*, Washington, 1911.

German Economy

rank of England—the two were the most important industrial exporters of the world. In 1880 German foreign trade ranked fourth among the exporting nations, that is, after Great Britain, France, and the United States. Soon Germany gained second place (after the United States only), a position which it maintained up to the World War.

The growth of German foreign trade from the foundation of the Reich until the war is a good index of the headlong expansion of the German economy in the last two decades of this era. Table 4 shows that German exports doubled in the twenty-eight years from 1872 to 1900, and that they more than doubled again the following thirteen years.

TABLE 4

German Foreign Trade

(Without re-export; in marks)

	Exports	Imports
1872	2,492,000,000	3,465,000,000
1880	2,977,000,000	2,844,000,000
1890	3,410,000,000	4,273,000,000
1900	4,753,000,000	6,043,000,000
1910	7,475,000,000	8,934,000,000
1913	10,097,000,000	10,770,000,000

Germany's rapid industrialization is reflected also in the composition of her foreign trade. The ratio of industrial finished products to total exports rose from 38 per

Toward Industrial World Power

cent in 1873 to 63 per cent in 1913. But the industrial affluence and the exporting capacity of the country were entirely dependent upon the importation of raw materials and foodstuffs, which by far exceeded the exports of finished goods. As Table 5 shows, this is true for the earlier as well as for the later stages.

TABLE 5

German Foreign Trade

	Exports	Imports	
	Semifinished and finished products	*Foodstuffs*	*Raw materials*
1890	2,148,000,000	1,397,000,000	1,797,000,000
1913	7,536,000,000	3,049,000,000	5,003,000,000

THE BANKS AS INSTRUMENTS OF FOREIGN TRADE AND CAPITAL EXPORT

Foreign trade of such huge dimensions requires adequate financing facilities. It was inevitable that gradually Germany should make every effort to break loose from the British financing system, which had a practical monopoly in international trade.

The concentrated efforts of the German banks to build up international connections date from the foundation of the Reich, but individual bankers had cultivated foreign relations even earlier. For instance, there

53

German Economy

was a personal tie between the Frankfort and New York houses of Speyer, later extended to the London house. In 1871, one year after its foundation, the Deutsche Bank took an interest in a London bank, and in 1873 it started a branch in London. Other German banks followed suit. In 1871 German banks took an interest in Belgian banks. In Italy the Banca Commerciale Italiana, one of the few big banks of the country, was founded in 1894 under the control of German banks; in Austria the Mercur Bank was under the control of German banking capital. Connection with the United States was cultivated primarily by German private bankers who established themselves in New York, such as Hallgarten & Co. and Ladenburg, Thalman & Co. The most notable of these connections was the one between the Hamburg house of M. M. Warburg & Co., founded in 1798, and the New York house of Kuhn, Loeb & Co.

The main purpose of these banking connections with the western European countries was to finance foreign trade. But the relations with American bankers were chiefly actuated by the desire to invest German capital in the United States. The same motives actuated the making of banking connections with more backward countries. A growing amount of American securities were placed in Germany, and the expansion of American railroads in particular was to a substantial extent financed by German capital.

Toward Industrial World Power

The efforts of German banks to establish foreign branches for the investment of capital abroad centered primarily in three geographical zones: the Near East, Latin America, and the Far East.

In the Near East the Deutsche Orientbank, founded by German banks in 1906, deserves to be mentioned first. It ran several branches in commercial centers of prewar Turkey, as well as in Egypt and Morocco. The German banks found another field of activity in Rumania, which was of particular interest to them because of her rich oil deposits. As early as 1890 the Darmstädter Bank took an interest in the Banca Marmarosch, which in due time became one of the leading Rumanian banks. The Disconto-Gesellschaft played a leading part in the organization of the Banca Generala Romana in 1897.

In the Far East the chief center of influence for German banking capital was the Deutsch-Asiatische Bank, founded in 1889 by a group of German banks under the leadership of the Disconto-Gesellschaft. The bank received the right of note issue for China, and expanded its influence as far as Japan and India.

In Latin America, finally, two powerful banking organizations carried forward the influence of German capital; first, the Deutsche Ueberseebank, a subsidiary of the Deutsche Bank founded in 1886; second, the Deutsch-Südamerikanische Bank, founded in 1906 under the auspices of the Dresdner Bank. Both banks estab-

German Economy

lished a far-flung net of branch institutions, partly under their own firm, partly under the firm of subsidiaries, which embraced almost every Latin American country, including Mexico.

GERMAN CAPITAL INVESTMENTS ABROAD

The branching out of German banks abroad denotes a tremendous outflow of German capital to foreign countries. In the 1880's Germany underwent a transition from a capital-importing to a capital-exporting country similar to that of the United States during the World War—although with several characteristic differences. In the first place, capital imports into Germany had never attained such dimensions as those into the United States. Furthermore, the heavy capital imports to Germany in the 1870's were of purely political origin (the French war indemnities), although their effect was naturally similar to an influx for economic reasons. Finally, in contrast to the United States, Germany's transition from a capital-importing to a capital-exporting country was not due to an increased export of war supplies, but was achieved despite a considerable import surplus. The explanation is that before the war, owing to Germany's rapid industrialization, the invisible balance of payments was heavily in her favor, primarily due to the proceeds of German shipping, to her geographical position in the center of European railway

56

Toward Industrial World Power

traffic, to services and profits of German foreign banks, and to the sale of German patents abroad.

German capital investments in other countries appeared under various headings. German companies founded foreign commercial organizations and industrial plants; German capital participated in foreign companies and purchased foreign securities; finally, after the 1880's German banks began to underwrite foreign capital issues in Germany. In the 1880's these foreign issues in Germany were considerable, but they diminished later with the growing capital needs of German industry. Still, during this entire period they never amounted to less than 400,000,000 marks a year. In all, between 1886 and 1912, 10,600,000,000 marks of foreign securities were issued in Germany.

For the last year before the World War the best estimates of German capital investments abroad give a total of approximately 30,000,000,000 marks, while there were 5,000,000,000 marks of foreign capital investments in Germany. It is safe to assume that German holdings of foreign securities reached about 20,000,000,000 marks, while the rest consisted of private, noncorporative investments. These estimates of foreign holdings are probably not too high, since the legal registration of foreign securities imposed by the German Government in 1916 revealed 16,248,000,000 marks. This leaves but a small margin for capital repatriated in the course of two war years, for capital that escaped to

German Economy

foreign countries, and for capital in Germany that failed to register.

DRANG NACH DEM OSTEN

German exports of industrial products and capital were instrumental in bringing about an economic and political expansion that, by its main orientation, gradually began to shift the balance of European power. In politically independent and strong countries like Russia, North America, and Latin America, German capital did not succeed in exerting much political influence. But in other capital-importing countries situated in a geographically and politically expedient radius of expansion, the economic influences could be aided and backed by political intervention. This is particularly true of southeastern Europe and Asia Minor, in fact, of those geographical regions traditionally exposed to the German *Drang nach dem Osten* (drive toward the East). There the chief goals of expansion were Austria-Hungary, Rumania, and Turkey. In the colonies, however, German capital found only unimportant investment opportunities.

In the Austro-Hungarian monarchy Germany functioned as pacemaker for the industrialization of the country. As in Rumania, German banks continued from the beginning of the century to be interested in the opening up of the oil fields in the Austrian province of Galicia (later a part of Poland). Soon after the founda-

Toward Industrial World Power

tion of the Reich, Austria-Hungary became the closest political ally of Germany. Rumania was primarily developed by German (and Austrian) capital, and was drawn into the immediate orbit of German power politics. Nevertheless, Rumania, after much hesitation, joined the Allies in 1916.

German expansion into Turkey coincided approximately with her expansion into Rumania. In Turkey German efforts were directed primarily toward the construction of railroads, which this poor country was unable to finance from its own resources. In 1899 the Deutsche Bank, together with an Austrian bank, acquired an interest in the Operating Company for Oriental Railways (Betriebsgesellschaft für Orientalische Eisenbahnen), which ran the Macedonian lines. In the same year the Deutsche Bank, jointly with the Dresdner Bank and other institutions, founded the Anatolian Railroad Company, which among others built the important line from Constantinople to Ankara. In the following year the Deutsche Bank participated in organizing the Bank for Oriental Railways formed in Zürich to finance the construction of the Anatolian Railroad. Finally, in 1901 the Sultan granted to the Anatolian Railroad Company the concession of historic fame for the construction of a railroad to Baghdad and the Persian Gulf. For the exploitation of this concession the Anatolian Railroad Company founded the Imperial Ottomanic

German Economy

Baghdad Railroad Company (Kaiserlich-Ottomanische Bagdad Bahngesellschaft).

In carrying her ventures into Asia Minor and threatening to extend them to the Persian Gulf, Germany made a deep inroad into the sphere of interest of the British Empire. It is widely known how the expanding German Empire crossed British interests in various other ways, chiefly by rapidly assuming a leading position in world trade and by building up the German Navy. Nevertheless, all these trends afford no factual evidence for the oft-repeated theory that it was primarily the economic rivalry between Germany and England that in the last analysis brought about the catastrophe of the World War. England would very likely have tolerated German expansion into Asia Minor, merely counteracting it by increasing her own naval armament to keep abreast of German armament. Europe was to be thrown out of its very precarious balance at another place.

6. FROM LIBERALISM TO PROTECTIONISM

It is well known that German unification was achieved when the half-feudalistic and militaristic Prussia established its sway over all Germany. But it should not be overlooked that inside Prussia—and more so in the other German states—liberal forces were so powerful that the dynasty never succeeded in eliminating them entirely.

Toward Industrial World Power

And it would be a real mistake to believe that the economic creed dominant when the Reich was founded was nationalistic and autarchic.

It has been noted above that the adoption of the gold standard was a reflection of the "Western liberal orientation." This orientation pervaded the entire economic policy in the era of the creation of the Reich. Von Delbrück, the Minister who determined Prussian trade policy after the revolution of 1848 and German trade policy after 1871, was a liberal freetrader. His whole attitude was dominated by this spirit, which was then fully endorsed by Bismarck. In the 1860's and the early 1870's business activities were freed from all sorts of legal and administrative restrictions. In 1870 the licensing system for stock companies was abolished, at first without even laying down any obligatory regulations for their charters and bylaws.

After the establishment of the Zollverein, protectionist tendencies began to play a role in German trade policy under the influence of the devastating competition from the English textile industry and under the spiritual influence of the great German economist Friedrich von List, the principal champion of the Zollverein idea. Consequently, a number of duties were imposed in the 1840's. But in the 1860's the trade policy of Europe generally reverted to liberal principles, that is, to lower tariffs and the most-favored-nation clause.

61

German Economy

TOWARD A FREE-TRADE POLICY

The turn was definitely achieved by the famous Cobden Treaty signed in 1860 between England and France. Prussia followed along the same line at once, and concluded a trade pact with France in 1862, also based on the most-favored-nation clause. This Prussian-French trade pact was destined to be of great importance later. Adopted in 1865 by the Zollverein, it became the pattern for several trade treaties concluded about that time by the Zollverein with other commercially important countries, for example, Great Britain, Austria, and Belgium. All these treaties contained the most-favored-nation clause, which implied a reduction in a great number of duties and the elimination of all agricultural duties.

The foundation of the Reich was at first even followed by a consolidation of the free-trade course. The trade treaty with France had been annulled by the War of 1870-71. In its place the famous paragraph was inserted in the Frankfort Peace Treaty providing for an "eternal" irrevocable mutual most-favored-nation clause, without allowing for duty limitations. This clause was to apply to all commercial treaties made by either country with other countries. This was in 1871. Two years later Germany abolished the duties on pig iron, scrap iron, and shipbuilding material and lowered the duties on half-finished iron products and machinery

62

Toward Industrial World Power

with the proviso that after 1877 the latter duties were to lapse entirely.

THE TURN TO PROTECTIONISM

Meanwhile, however, the fundamental change slowly emerged that was to become of the greatest consequence for German history in the following years. In 1873 the speculative boom exploded, and a deep and persistent depression settled on German business. In the same year the iron duties were abolished. But there was depression in England also, and therefore England, still superior in technical skill, flooded the German market with iron and iron products at prices that made it impossible for German heavy industries to compete. At the same time, German textile industries were exposed to the superior competition of Alsace-Lorraine, which they now had to face without protection. Finally, in German agriculture the turning-point was near at hand, after which this traditional export industry was transformed into the vulnerable import industry of the later period. Although as late as from 1876 to 1879, the German Agricultural Council (Landwirtschaftsrat) pleaded for adherence to free trade for agricultural products, these years brought simultaneously the final decision in western and central Europe for intensive agriculture and in the rest of the world, primarily in the United States, that for extensive agriculture. Since the 1820's German agriculture had

German Economy

progressed remarkably, helped by British experience, and by the epoch-making researches of Von Liebig. From the extensive triennial crop rotation (which in every year left one-third of arable space fallow) German agriculture had progressed to the intensive crop-rotation system by means of fertilizers.

But intensive farming on soil kept under cultivation for generations means rising costs per unit, if compared with the extensive methods of eastern Europe, and even higher costs compared with farming on the virgin soil overseas. The trend toward rising production costs in Germany clashed with the opposite trend toward lower costs in overseas countries, and in the 1870's these two converse curves crossed each other. It was especially the American grain that was now dumped on the open German market, strongly favored as to transportation costs by the rapid development of the railway systems on the North American continent and by the growing competition of the transatlantic steamship lines. Germany, the classical grain-exporting country, was rapidly transformed into an import market. Already in 1879-80, 324,000 tons of wheat and 160,000 tons of corn were imported from the United States, and additional grain from Hungary and Russia.

Thus all conditions coincided in Germany to uproot the free-trade ideology: the strain of the world-wide depression; the change in the international agricultural situation; the progress of British iron, which threatened

Toward Industrial World Power

to stifle the flourishing German iron industry. It was this concentric pressure, not the triumph of Bismarckian Prussia over Germany, that brought about the gradual collapse of the free-trade policy in Germany. For, to emphasize this fact once more, Bismarck and the social stratum of his origin, the Prussian Junkers, were free-traders originally and became protectionists only under the strain of the altered situation of the 1870's.

Things came to such a pass that in 1876 Von Delbrück, then president of the Chancellor's office, resigned, not on account of divergencies in tariff policies, but over railway controversies. Even so, his resignation was symptomatic of the incipient fundamental change in German economic policies and ideologies. The propaganda in favor of a shift in tariffs had already begun to work, and only three years later, in 1879, the change was actually initiated. The new Tariff Bill, enacted in 1879-80, reintroduced agricultural duties, iron duties, and several industrial duties, and increased textile and other industrial duties.

These duties, however, remained very moderate, at least measured by more recent standards. The duty on wheat and rye was only 10 marks per ton, not quite 5 per cent of the value. The iron duty was the same, but was somewhat higher in proportion to the price. Only in the course of the following years, after it had become evident that the low tariff had failed to halt the decline in German grain prices, were the grain duties

German Economy

raised to a higher level. In 1887 the wheat and rye duties had gradually been raised to 50 marks per ton, and still the average price for German grain was lower than it was before the duties were first introduced.

To complete the history of German tariff policies before the World War, it should be noted that the German protectionist trend was not pursued without hesitation. Bismarck's dismissal in 1890 was indicative of a turn, although a short-lived one, to the Left, in politics as well as in economics. Bismarck was followed by Caprivi. The Anti-Socialist Laws were repealed, and the agricultural and several industrial duties were lowered, with the object of inducing other countries to lower their tariffs on German industrial products.

But the "Caprivi era" proved to be merely a brief episode. In 1902, under Prince von Bülow's chancellorship, the tariff was again raised. It should, however, be emphasized that even then, and up to the World War, the German tariff remained relatively moderate. It was moderate compared with the levels reached after the war and also moderate compared with contemporaneous tariffs in the United States, France, Austria, and Russia, which also had the same or lesser industrial aspirations. Even after 1879, when German foreign-trade policies veered toward protectionism, prewar Germany was neither in fact nor in ideology actuated by autarchical aims.

Toward Industrial World Power

7. THE COLONIAL ERA

Bismarck's Prussia was a military, not a naval, state. Hamburg and Bremen, Germany's outlets to the world at large, were not Prussian and did not even belong to the German Zollverein. The Prussian ports of Danzig and Königsberg were situated far back on the Baltic Sea, which, especially before the construction of the Kaiser Wilhelm Canal, was obviously an inland sea. Prussia's aspirations were centered on continental Europe exclusively. Bismarck himself was originally a declared enemy of the "colonial idea." This not only appears from his private correspondence just before the Franco-Prussian War, but is also proved by the fact that Germany as late as 1874 declined to consider an appeal for German protection coming from the Sultan of Zanzibar and thus missed a favorable chance to lay the foundation for a colonial empire in the region where ten years later one of the most important German colonial enterprises was to be built up. But when the turn in foreign-trade policy occurred, Germany modified her attitude toward colonial problems; the "colonial idea" made its entry.

One may, of course, argue that this was only a natural change, the inevitable consequence of Germany's advancing industrialization and of the incorporation of the great ports, Hamburg and Bremen, into the Reich. One may also point out that for centuries other European states had preceded Germany on the path to co-

German Economy

lonial empires, and that precisely in the period following the Franco-Prussian War, France, as well as Belgium and Portugal, was feverishly active in the colonial sphere. And finally one could point to the huge German emigration, which, as shown above, turned almost exclusively to the United States, where sooner or later the emigrants were lost to the German nation.

Undoubtedly, there is much truth in all these contentions. But it is also true that the German colonies were never of much consequence for the expansionist needs of German industries and never became potential outlets for German emigration.

As to German emigration, it began to dwindle just in the period of German colonial successes. But even if this had not happened, the German colonies would never have offered opportunities for the settlement of a large number of European emigrants. All the African colonies had been acquired in 1884 and 1885. In 1897 the ninety-nine years' "lease" of Kiaochow from China was added, and in 1899 and 1900 the Carolines and about half of Samoa were acquired in the Pacific. On the eve of the World War the German colonies had a total expanse of 1,135,000 square miles, with a population of more than 13,000,000. But after thirty years of colonizing activity, the number of whites in all the German colonies did not exceed 23,952, of whom as many as 5,764 were in military or police service.

The slender value of the German colonies for her

Toward Industrial World Power

economic life may be gleaned from the following facts: On the eve of the World War, German capital working in the colonies was a little over 500,000,000 marks, that is, not quite 2 per cent of German capital investments abroad. German capital was primarily employed in the colonies in building up a relatively dense railroad system (a total of 3,350 miles in 1914); also port facilities, plantations, and mines. The chief export commodities produced by the colonies were diamonds (Southwest Africa), rubber, and vegetable-oil products. Altogether exports did not exceed 83,600,000 marks in 1912. The colonies were, therefore, of no value for supplying German industry with raw materials, nor could they furnish a sizable market for German industries. In 1913, of total German exports, 10,097,000,000 marks, only 55,000,000 marks went into her own colonies (except Kiaochow)—that is, only one-half of 1 per cent.

After the appointment in 1906 of the banker Dr. Dernburg as chief of the German colonial administration and after he had organized the Colonial Office in 1907, increased effort was devoted to the economic development of the colonies. But the effect was not considerable, and it is doubtful whether it could have improved much even if German colonial power had not been broken up by the World War.

German Economy

8. GOVERNMENT OWNERSHIP

As in all other European countries, state help and state initiative for the development of industries were among the most important instruments in building up capitalism in Germany. As in other countries, state-owned "factories" (*Manufakturen*) were established in Germany during her mercantile era. Some of them remain state-owned enterprises to this day, for example, the Prussian and Saxonian porcelain factories. The special political character of Germany at that time favored this kind of state ownership. The several dozens of princes reigning since feudal times owned domains, forests, and also some industrial enterprises that were in fact state property, although many of them were officially considered as private property of the individual reigning houses.

Thus Germany entered the liberal era with a relatively large sector of state-controlled economy, and naturally this property was not liquidated in the pursuit of purely ideological considerations. But it was most significant for the future destiny of Germany that when she emerged from the liberal era, she could immediately revert to her old mercantilistic tradition and follow it with increasing impetus.

Toward Industrial World Power

THE NATIONALIZATION OF THE RAILROADS

The first and most important measure in this direction was the nationalization of the railroads. After 1835, when the first German railroad was built connecting the neighboring towns of Nuremberg and Fürth, and up to the World War, the tempo of development of the German railroad system must be considered as extraordinary when measured by European standards. As in other highly developed countries, the building of railroads stopped abruptly with the World War. The pace of railroad construction is shown in Table 6.

TABLE 6

German Railroads
(kilometers)

	Mileage in operation	Increase per decade
1835	6	
1845	2,300	2,300
1855	8,290	5,990
1865	14,690	6,400
1875	27,930	13,240
1885	37,650	9,720
1895	46,560	8,910
1905	56,980	10,420
1915	62,410	5,430

In some German states (Baden, Braunschweig, Württemberg, Oldenburg) railroad construction was taken up by the state from the very beginning. In others, as

German Economy

in Saxony and Bavaria, part of the railroad system was state-owned or was later purchased by the state. But in Prussia, initially (1838) the state was content with instituting an extensive supervision over the railroads, reserving the right to acquire them after thirty years. Railroad construction itself remained in private hands, and not until 1847 did the Prussian state begin to build some lines on its own. By the annexation of Hanover and several other territories in 1866 Prussia acquired some other state lines. The Reich itself (up to the Weimar Constitution) acquired only one state railroad, the Alsace-Lorraine system. That became Reich property in 1871.

In 1875, however, on the eve of the great period of nationalization, approximately one-half of the German railroad system was still in private hands. And it was in the first half of the 1870's that private railroad construction expanded most rapidly. This was the main field of activity in the promoters' era. Table 6 shows that in the one decade from 1865 to 1875 the German railroad system almost doubled. But railway stocks were also the main object of the speculative bubble, and when in 1873 the great crash came, countless bona-fide investors found themselves robbed of their savings invested in railroad "securities."

It would certainly have been possible to prevent future promotional frauds, unsound business practices, and chaotic developments by other methods than outright

Toward Industrial World Power

nationalization of railroads. But noneconomic considerations, primarily military, played an important part in the discussion. It is characteristic of this situation that Bismarck personally advocated the nationalization of the railroads, while his liberal Minister Delbrück opposed it. As mentioned before, it was this difference of opinion that led to Delbrück's resignation in 1876. From then on the path to nationalization lay open. And it is again characteristic that the nationalization scheme was adopted in precisely the year when the great turn toward protectionism occurred.

Nationalization was carried out—first by Prussia—by purchasing the private roads on the basis of provisions contained in the original charters. The governments raised the money by issuing bonds to replace the bond issues of the railroad companies. In 1875, of a total network of 27,956 kilometers, 12,062 kilometers were state-owned, 3,253 kilometers were operated by private companies under state management, and 12,641 kilometers were operated by private companies under private management. In 1912, of a total network of 60,521 kilometers, only 3,631 kilometers were privately owned (and of these only 277 kilometers represented main lines).

It should be remembered, however, that one of the advantages usually derived from the nationalization of a railroad system could not be realized completely in Germany up to the Weimar period; namely, the unifi-

German Economy

cation of the system. Apart from the private roads, eight state-owned systems were in operation. The largest was managed jointly by Prussia and Hesse; six systems belonged to other federal states; and one belonged to the Reich. The constitution of the North German Federation, and subsequently the constitution of Bismarck's Reich, put the Reich in supreme control over all railroads, and after 1877 the railroad services were unified as to many technical details. However, Bismarck's early plan of 1866 to bring all railroads under Reich ownership was defeated by opposing federalistic forces. As a result, Reich control over the railroads turned out to be much weaker than the powers that devolved upon the United States after the Interstate Commerce Commission was formed. The relationship between the eight public railroad systems was more or less what it would have been among private systems under a loose state supervision.

At last the Weimar Constitution achieved full unification of the German railroad system by providing that all state railroads should be transferred to the Reich. This transfer of ownership was executed by contractual arrangements between the Reich and the eight railroad-owning states. The Reich thereby acquired a railroad system of more than 53,000 kilometers.

Toward Industrial World Power

HEAVY INDUSTRIES, PUBLIC UTILITIES, BANKS

After the nationalization of the railroads state entrepreneurial activities in many other fields of business grew apace. The federal states as well as the municipalities participated most actively in the development of industries, chiefly state-owned mines and ironworks. Thus, for instance, at the beginning of the World War the Prussian state owned some forty mines and twelve blast furnaces. The slogan of "municipal socialism" began its sway in the Imperial era, not waiting for the Weimar Republic. The rapidly growing cities "socialized" electric plants, gasworks and waterworks, traction companies, and slaughterhouses in increasing number, or erected new plants under their ownership.

Apart from the plants that were entirely publicly owned, so-called mixed-ownership companies (*gemischt-wirtschaftliche Gesellschaften*) originated beginning with the twentieth century. They were under the joint control of private capital and public authorities. This kind of organization was tried out chiefly among public utilities, such as electric plants, gasworks and waterworks, and traction systems. In these companies, usually formed at the initiative of private entrepreneurs, the municipalities then acquired stock interests, as a rule in exchange for the granting of franchises. The most important example of such an enterprise is the Rheinisch-Westfälische Elektrizitätswerke located in Germany's

German Economy

foremost industrial center, which provided several industrial cities with their electric power. It had been formed by private capital in 1905, but the consumer cities were given a share in its management. Local distribution in most cases was by municipal companies, which bought the power wholesale and derived very substantial profits from this business. This soon came to be one of the important sources of municipal revenues.

From the monarchy the Republic inherited a typically "mixed-ownership" economic system in which the sector of state ownership as a whole did not rank far behind the private sector. On the eve of the World War the following services were entirely state-owned: postal, telephone, telegraph (with the exception of overseas telegraph systems, which were in private hands), and railroads. Almost fully under municipal or "mixed ownership" were the gasworks and waterworks and the traction systems. Power production was predominantly under municipal, state, or "mixed" ownership.

The state played an important role also in the banking system, even apart from the central bank, which held a far greater position inside Germany's economic system than was true of the countries with an Anglo-Saxon banking system. The stock of the Reichsbank was in private hands, but its president and other officers were appointed by the Kaiser, and the stockholders had no rights in the conduct of affairs, no influence on the policy of the bank. Besides the Reichsbank there were

Toward Industrial World Power

several powerful state banks, all of which played a dominant role in the Berlin money market. Among them the strongest was the Prussian State Bank (Preussische Seehandlung), founded as early as 1772. Furthermore, practically the whole savings-bank system was municipal. This was important, because the savings banks had to handle far greater funds than all the credit banks put together.

To round out the picture, we may add that the proportion of mines and other industrial enterprises under state management was very considerable, that state and municipal ownerships were dominant in forestry, and that even among the large-scale farms state-owned units had some importance. Imperial Germany had gradually become an economic system of mixed private and public ownership. In this era the foundations were already laid on which later the war economy, the experiments of the Republic, and finally the National Socialist system could be built.

9. SOCIAL REFORM

The idea of social reform originated in countries with older industrial traditions, primarily in England, not in Germany. Social reform was meant to brake the forces of capitalism wherever their full sway could breed or had bred obvious social defects. But in no other country had the idea of social reform impressed the minds of the

German Economy

people so deeply as in Germany, or been carried so fully to the point of a whole social philosophy. The movement took hold of the universities, it was represented by the so-called Professorial Socialism (*Kathedersozialismus*), whose influence was so deeply rooted that the glamour of the renowned association of social scholars founded in 1872 under the name of Verein für Sozialpolitik (Association for Social Policy) was still fresh when the National Socialist regime wiped it out. In the churches Christian Socialist movements developed (their chief exponent being the Catholic Bishop Ketteler), and it culminated in the formation of the Christian trade-unions.

In Germany, more than in any other country, it was the state that first adopted the idea of social reforms and became active in this field. Two distinct motives shaped the social program of that period: (1) the common protectionist ideology dominant in German policy since the second half of the 1870's, and (2) the competition with the vigorously rising Socialist movement. It is deeply significant that the whole system of social insurance, which by one stroke made Germany the leader in social reform throughout the civilized world, was built up in the era of the Anti-Socialist Laws.

In 1878 the reaction against the liberal era had advanced so far that Bismarck conceived the infelicitous plan of stifling the powerfully developing Socialist movement by emergency legislation. In 1878 there were two

Toward Industrial World Power

unsuccessful attempts on the life of the old Kaiser William I. The perpetrators were proved to be individuals entirely unconnected with the Socialist party. These attempts were made a pretext, however, for setting in force the Anti-Socialist Act, which denied the Socialist party and the affiliated unions any legal activity. The *Gesetz gegen die gemeingefährlichen Bestrebungen der Sozialdemokratie* (Act against the Aims of Social Democracy Dangerous to the Commonwealth) went into effect on October 1, 1878. Under this act, Socialist associations were to be dissolved and their funds seized. Persons who professionally propagated Socialist or Communist ideas could be restricted in the choice of their domicile and in their free movement. The police authorities were empowered to forbid or dissolve meetings and to confiscate or suppress printed matter. The Social-Democratic party submitted to this law with perfect discipline, and reported to the police the dissolution of their party organizations. The effects of the law, dubious from the beginning, became wholly negative as time went on. There were only nine Social-Democratic members of the Reichstag left. But they formed a nucleus sufficient for a future reorganization of the party. The party created a publishing house in Zürich, Switzerland, which published the official party newspaper, *Der Sozialdemokrat*, and also forbidden pamphlets and books. Eduard Bernstein served as editor. It is significant for the relatively liberal atmosphere of this era, as compared with

German Economy

the oppressive methods of modern dictatorships, that there was not much difficulty in smuggling into Germany from Switzerland either the newspaper or other publications.

Nevertheless, in the first two years about a thousand persons were forcibly removed from a few big cities, and a hundred and fifty periodicals and roughly a thousand books and pamphlets were suppressed. A few hundred persons were sentenced to prison for lese majesty. Despite these persecutions, at the Reichstag elections of 1881 the party increased the number of its representatives from 9 to 12, and the party was rebuilt in camouflaged organizations. Glee clubs, bowling clubs, charity associations, and so on served this purpose. From London, Friedrich Engels sent money and thereby strengthened his radicalizing influence. Thus, by the end of the 1880's the Hamburg organization alone numbered about 6,000 members, and when at the elections of 1890 the number of votes doubled and the number of deputies quadrupled as compared with 1878, the time seemed ripe for the young Emperor William II to let the Anti-Socialist Act lapse. Bismarck had been dismissed a few months before, and his insistence on an extension of the Anti-Socialist Act was an important point in his conflict with the Emperor.

In 1883, five years after the Anti-Socialist Laws had been enacted, the first social-insurance law came into force. Based on previous voluntary arrangements, it

Toward Industrial World Power

provided for a compulsory health insurance for workers. Accident insurance for workers was organized the next year, followed in 1889 by old-age and sickness insurance, with which the foundations of this whole legislative structure were completed as far as the Imperial era was concerned.

Thus among the workers of all countries the German workers were the first to be protected against the worst social dangers to which they were exposed—with the exception of unemployment, which, while Germany continued her spectacular economic progress, was not yet viewed as a common and dangerous social evil. If a worker or his wife or child fell ill, the health-insurance fund provided adequate medical and financial aid, placed them in hospitals or sanitariums, and provided for their medicine. Whenever a worker had an accident, the compensation fund took over all medical costs. Whenever he became partly or totally disabled, and after he had reached his sixty-fifth year, he received a pension providing an adequate living. If he died before reaching sixty-five years of age, his widow and orphans were entitled to an annuity.

The costs of accident insurance were borne by the employer alone; those of health insurance were shared by employer and employee; in the old-age and sickness insurance the Reich was from the beginning the third participant. According to their contributions, employers and employees had a share in the autonomous man-

German Economy

agement of the social-insurance institutions. Of course, this feature of self-government, together with all other forms of self-government, disappeared later under the National Socialist regime.

Workers' protection was not confined to social insurance. Immediately after Bismarck's resignation in 1891 the first important protective legislation for workers was enacted. It provided for a maximum working day of 11 hours for women and 10 hours for children, prohibited night work for women and children and any kind of employment of children under fourteen in industry and trade, and made a free Sunday and various hygienic rules obligatory. This was followed by other protective legislation.

But social reform did not end with the working class. Gradually it became evident that the industrial middle classes too were entitled to some protection. The guilds, which had lost their legal standing in the new Trades Code, began to be legally regulated again after 1878. Finally in 1897, by reintroducing guilds with compulsory membership for most crafts, the principle of free competition was largely abandoned in the field of crafts. By this law of 1897 the local authorities were empowered to unite craft groups into compulsory guilds, which were given the right of regulating production, fixing prices, training apprentices, and so forth. In 1904 more than half of all guilds were compulsory guilds.

Toward Industrial World Power

10. THE ORGANIZATION OF BUSINESS AND LABOR

The compulsory guilds were a kind of cartel for the crafts instituted by law. When they were first set up, industrial cartels were already in existence. But only after 1879 did the German cartels become widespread and characteristic of the whole of German industrial life. In fact, modern industrial cartels are of German origin, and one cannot understand the peculiar development of Germany, either politically or economically, without clarifying their significance.

THE CARTELIZATION OF INDUSTRY

The trend of modern industrialism has been determined in all countries by two conflicting tendencies: the one toward liberation of the individual from ties and codes inherited from the Middle Ages and the mercantilistic era; the other toward integration on a more or less monopolistic basis. The whole Western world has experienced this conflict. But, with the sole exception of Germany, the individualistic tendency was defended by the policies of the various countries, and monopolies were torn up or at least made as difficult as possible. The Anti-Trust Laws in the United States were the extreme expression of this individualistic philosophy. Free competition was the only recognized economic policy. In-

German Economy

fringement of free competition was made a criminal offense. The western European countries did not go as far as that. But England, France, Austria, and, following them, the smaller industrialized countries declared agreements in restraint of trade void and therefore unenforceable in the courts. In Germany alone cartel agreements had "legal status"; that is, they were treated by the law like any other private contracts. Any contravention of the contractual provisions among members of a cartel could be brought into court or penalized by the forfeiture of bonds provided for this purpose under the agreement. Not until 1923, at the end of the inflation period, was a cartel law enacted. This we shall have to deal with in a subsequent chapter.

Nothing shows more clearly how little liberalism had taken root in the German mind than this special treatment of cartels. Liberalism was never recognized as the basis of a free capitalist system. As early as 1883, Professor Kleinwächter, an Austrian economist, who wrote the first scientific book on cartels, approved them as "the pioneer foundation of a state-controlled economy." The mercantilistic spirit, which all too readily merged later with the collectivist spirit of the labor movement, was strong even in the liberal era. The result of this merger was Hitlerism. In this liberal era the profit motive (which is basic to free competition) was not regarded as either desirable or honorable even by the ruling classes. The bureaucracy and the army, which

Toward Industrial World Power

set the tone, looked at it as something rather contemptible, and the capitalistic bourgeoisie adjusted itself to the ideologies of the noneconomic classes. The antithesis of *Jobbers and Heroes (Händler und Helden)*, the title of a widely read World War pamphlet by Professor Sombart, emphasized the existing contrast between the Anglo-Saxon and German "mentalities."

The cartelization of Germany, however, did not progress along a continuous line. Years of expansion were followed by years in which the cartels disintegrated. As a rule it may be stated that cartels in Germany were the outgrowth of depressions. Whenever prices tended to drop below costs, cartels were founded in order to keep business "in the black." When the depression was followed by prosperity, the more successful entrepreneurs got tired of the restrictions imposed on them by the cartels and tried to get rid of them.

In the history of the cartels, as in so many other respects, 1879 marked the turning-point, the year when German tariff policy turned toward protectionism. Only under the protection of a tariff wall could cartel agreements become effective. Competition among domestic producers of a commodity has to be eliminated in order to enable them to fructify the whole difference between foreign and domestic prices made possible by the tariff. The first cartels were formed for coke, pig iron, and steel sheets. Perhaps the most important one for its principle, the Potash Syndicate, was founded in

German Economy

1881. It represented the first experiment in monopolistic exploitation of a basic raw material, and it concerned the one natural resource in which up to the World War Germany possessed a virtual world monopoly. In the potash industry in 1910 the Government enforced the first compulsory industrial cartel, primarily for the purpose of organized exploitation of the American market, which had to pay more for potash than the German domestic price. Materially more important for Germany was a combination in the Ruhr coal-mining organized in 1897 through the Rhenish-Westphalian Coal Syndicate. At the same time the various branches of the steel industry began to form combines, a process that culminated (before the World War) in the formation of the Steel Works Association (Stahlwerksverband) in 1904. German industries also very early played a leading part in international cartels. The first important one was the Irma (International Rail Makers Association), founded in 1883 by British, German, and Belgian steel mills and later joined by the French. The object was to distribute world markets among the various groups of producers.

By the middle of the 1890's, besides steel and coal, plate glass, cement, and certain chemicals were organized in cartels. But the great era of almost general cartelization of German industry came after the turn of the century. The attack against free individual competition was launched both through giant mergers—partic-

Toward Industrial World Power

ularly in the heavy industries—and through nation-wide cartelization. At the outbreak of the war in 1914 the German cartel system was essentially completed.

But the word "cartel" covered combines of a very variegated sort. There were the strictest organizations that syndicated the sale of certain products by centralized sales offices outside of which no purchases and sales could be made. Production was distributed by quota among the member-producers, and the only entrepreneurial activity left to the individual producer was the care for technical efficiency and thereby for reduction of costs and increase of the profit margin at a unified price level. But this sort of complete centralization was rather the exception, although the rule in most of the basic industries. The thousands of cartels into which most German business eventually was organized were much looser formations. Some fixed production quotas without centralization of sales; others distributed regional markets assigned to the individual producers; others only regulated conditions and terms of sales, as for instance limitation of credits, or issued rules for calculation of costs (to prevent "cutthroat competition"), and so on.

The history of German cartelization is also the history of continual struggles within the cartels. At every renewal of an expiring cartel agreement fights flared up both against outsiders who had come up in the meantime and among the members themselves, who tried to

87

German Economy

enlarge their quotas at the expense of their fellow members. Time and again these fights degenerated into disruption of cartels, price cuts, and the like, but in many cases with the benevolent support of the Government peace was re-established in a new agreement. Thus cartelization was the basis on which the war economy in the first World War could easily be predicated. Eventually the totalitarian economic system of the Third Reich employed it on an even higher scale for its own purposes.

THE FLOWERING OF TRADE-UNIONS

As had been the case in England, the German workers were long prohibited by antiunion legislation from organizing in trade-unions. Only after the liberal era of the 1860's was well under way were most of these restrictions allowed to lapse. First among the German federal states to repeal the antiorganization laws was highly industrialized Saxony (in 1861). In 1869 the North German Federation followed by enacting the Trades Code, which granted freedom of organization, at least to industrial workers. This Trades Code was adopted by the Reich in 1871.

Immediately after the disappearance of these legal barriers the first trade-unions were formed, and as early as 1865 and 1866 national organizations of tobacco workers and printers were set up. In marked contrast to unions in the Anglo-Saxon countries, the German

Toward Industrial World Power

unions were built up by central organizations that were decidedly political in character. In 1868 no less than three experiments were made to form a centralized union of unions. One of these experiments, at the time the most important of the three, was initiated by the leader of the Lassalle group of unions, J. von Schweitzer. The second, later destined to be of the greatest importance, was made by August Bebel, the leader of the Marxist International Workers' Association. The third was made by two leaders of the Progressive party, Max Hirsch and Franz Duncker. All three were at first surprisingly successful. But soon the Schweitzer unions began to degenerate, and after Lassalle's and the Marxist movement had merged, they joined the Marxist unions. The Hirsch-Duncker Unions remained in existence up to the end of the Weimar Republic, but they never gained much importance. In 1899 a third group of unions became active: the Christian Unions, a combination of localized organizations formed in the 1890's by Roman Catholic, and in smaller part by Protestant, workers' associations.

Thus from its beginning to its end in 1933 the German trade-union movement was politically oriented. The Free Unions, the name later adopted by the main union body, were affiliated with the Social-Democratic party. The Christian Unions, despite their denominationally mixed membership, were affiliated with the Center party, and the Hirsch-Duncker Unions with the

German Economy

liberal parties. Later, especially in the period of the Anti-Socialist Laws, the contact between the Free Unions and the Social-Democratic party was for a time somewhat loosened. By these laws union activities were declared illegal, as were party activities. But soon organizations reappeared under the guise of nonpolitical "craft associations," and in 1884 they regained the status of unions. In 1890, as soon as the Anti-Socialist Laws were repealed, the Free Unions formed a General Commission independent of the Social-Democratic party. This continued to be the central organization of the Free Unions, merely changing its name after the World War to Allgemeiner Deutscher Gewerkschaftsbund (General German League of Unions).

With the repeal of the anti-Socialist legislation, the uninterrupted growth of the unions began. The Free Unions increased their membership from about 300,000 in 1890 to 2,500,000 in 1914, and the other union groups had a proportionate development. Table 7 shows the total number of trade-unionists at the end of the prewar period (1913).

TABLE 7

German Trade-Unions

Free Unions	2,525,000
Christian Unions	342,000
Hirsch-Duncker Unions	107,000
Independent associations	319,000
Total	3,293,000

Toward Industrial World Power

This unionization was paralleled by similar activities among the employers, who also formed centralized associations. In the entire prewar era the relations between employers and employees remained predominantly an autonomous affair of these groups. The state kept out completely, except of course for the protection that civil law accorded industrial agreements as well as all other kinds of contracts. The industrial courts formed in 1891, however, were the first step in the direction of state regulation of employer-employee relations. But beyond that, relations between employers or their associations and trade-unions were not much regulated before the war. The whole technique of collective agreements developed very slowly, and the number of such agreements remained small. The rapid upsurge of German industry and the relative mildness of the business cycles of that period on both the up and the down swings helped to keep labor troubles within moderate limits as to the number and intensity of strifes.

THE CO-OPERATIVES

Together with the cartels and trade-unions the co-operatives also built up their mighty organizations. Following the British example, consumers' co-operatives were formed, which, in both membership and activities —extending even into the sphere of production—were second only to the British organizations of the same

German Economy

kind. For small tradesmen the ideas of Schulze-Delitzsch, for farmers those of Raiffeisen, became of decisive importance. Both these main groups of the middle class found much economic support in co-operative organizations, primarily in credit associations for traders and farmers respectively. Buying and selling co-operatives were also formed, chiefly in the agricultural field.

Thus Germany, as long ago as the last decades before the World War—well before the period of Weimar and of National Socialism—developed the basic features of an economic system very different from the so-called classical liberal system on which the Bismarckian era had embarked in accordance with the western-European pattern. Even in its resplendent time German capitalism showed a generous admixture of state and association control of business.

PART III

THE WORLD WAR

THE WORLD WAR

I. WAR FINANCES

GERMANY'S PHENOMENAL RISE to an industrial World Power, well-balanced both within herself and as a member of the world economy, was destroyed by a sudden catastrophe. The World War convulsed the whole world, but in none of the other leading industrial nations was the revolution of the entire economic, social, and political structure as fundamental and lasting as in Germany. It is true that for four long and terrific years the actors who had dominated the German scene for the preceding forty years continued to perform. Indeed, as viewed from the outside, these four years could even be taken to bring the ultimate fulfillment, the utmost accomplishment, of the old system. But in reality, what was going on in Germany during the World War was already something intrinsically new, even if the threads tying the present to the past seem strong enough to make the change at least comprehensible.

Not only had Germany and German industry the tremendous task of providing alone, without economic or financial help from abroad, for all armaments during four years of the greatest war ever fought in history, but also while the industrial nations on the other side of

German Economy

the trenches were able to call in the aid of the greatest economic World Power, the United States, Germany's fate was decisively altered by the blockade, which now forced her into an involuntary and inexorable autarchy, although up to that time she had participated in world trade more than any other nation except England. This experience has never faded from the memory of the German people. Without it the economic policy of the Hitler regime cannot be understood.

When the World War broke out on August 4, 1914 (the hostilities between Austria-Hungary and Serbia had begun one week earlier), Germany was economically completely unprepared for a war that was to expose her for several years to the immense endurance test of an economic and financial isolation. German statesmanship was obviously allowing only for a lightning campaign. Nothing was prepared for a struggle of many years with an adversary of equal strength, even less for the possibility and the consequences of a blockade. The First Battle of the Marne, which ended the German military dream, was also the Battle of the Marne for German war economy.

THE FINANCIAL MOBILIZATION

In one economic sphere alone did Germany have something like a plan according to which, in case of war, she could begin to act on the very first day: the

The World War

sphere of money and credit and of state finance. The German Government had not troubled their heads how, if the dreadful emergency came, they would procure bread for the people and raw materials for the army. But they had taken well to heart the old and wise adage that three things are indispensable to wage a modern war: money, money, and again money. It was soon to become apparent, however, that the money they could provide was not of much use in a modern war.

In the week from July 23 to July 31, 1914 (on July 23 the Austro-Hungarian Government presented a forty-eight-hour ultimatum to the Serbian Government), the Reichsbank lost more than 100,000,000 marks in gold, the gold reserve decreasing from 1,357,-000,000 to 1,253,000,000 marks. On the other hand, the note circulation of the Reichsbank increased from 1,891,000,000 to 2,909,000,000 marks. The hoarding of gold and the exchange of bank deposits into banknotes were conclusive symptoms that the war scare had taken hold of the public. On July 31, 1914, for the first time in its almost forty-year career, the Reichsbank discontinued the redemption of bank notes in gold, although it was legally obligatory. The note circulation was still covered by gold by as much as 43 per cent, and banknotes plus demand deposits by 30 per cent.[1]

[1] The gold-coverage requirements of the Reichsbank, 33⅓ per cent, referred to banknotes alone, not to other demand liabilities. It was accordingly not customary for the public to regard banknotes and other liabilities (check deposits) of the bank as essentially the same.

German Economy

In the memorable session for which the Reichstag assembled on August 4, 1914, it became evident not only that this suspension of gold payments constituted a measure of foresight to guard against the threatened panic, but also that this was the first step in a well-thought-out plan. The several financial bills put before the Reichstag were all enacted on that day. One of these laws authorized the Reich Government to borrow up to 5,000,000,000 marks for war purposes. It is commonly known that this was the formal act by which the German parliament, including the Social-Democratic representatives, sanctioned a war that had been decided upon over their heads by the prerogative of the monarch.

The law concerning the war credits was an enabling act such as every government needs in an emergency. For the moment, and also as typical of the German method of war financing, the other financial laws adopted on August 4, 1914, had greater importance. They provided:

1. That the redemption of banknotes (of the Reichsbank as well as of the private note banks) in gold should be suspended, or rather remain suspended after having been interrupted five days before.

2. That the tax on all note circulation in excess of 550,000,000 marks over and above the gold coverage was to be abolished.

The World War

3. That Loan Banks (*Darlehenskassen*) were to be organized.

4. That the Reichsbank was empowered to include three-month Treasury bills of the Reich in its note coverage, and "Loan Bank notes" (*Darlehenskassenscheine*) in its "ready-money coverage" (*Bardeckung*).

Of these four laws, the first can be explained as a purely defensive measure against gold-hoarding. In time of war the Government is in such urgent need of the centralized gold reserve that safeguards must be established against the danger of its being scattered. But by the other three laws the Government was definitely, though unconsciously, paving the way for future inflation.

The Loan Banks (*Darlehenskassen*) were a war institution organized for the first time during the Franco-Prussian War of 1870-71, at that time as an emergency measure to procure credits for business requirements. The same task devolved on the Loan Banks formed in 1914, which kept up their functions to the end of the inflation era in 1924. Apart from this, they were meant chiefly as a supplementary organization for the Reichsbank, having the advantage of being free from the restrictions by which this institution was still hampered. This was the beginning of the system of supplementary organizations for the Reichsbank that was to become characteristic of future German currency policies.

German Economy

The Loan Banks had the power to make loans on securities disqualified as collateral for loans by the Reichsbank. Besides, the Loan Banks extended credits to the federal states and municipalities as well as to war corporations (*Kriegsgesellschaften*), and finally it was their allotted task to make advances for subscriptions to the war loans. The funds of the Loan Banks were procured very simply by means of the printing press. So-called Loan Bank notes (*Darlehenskassenscheine*) were issued to the full amount of the outstanding credits of the Loan Banks; they were regarded as legal tender, and were in part taken up by the Reichsbank, in part put immediately into circulation.

But the most important step toward unrestrained inflation was prepared by the clause that empowered the Reichsbank to rediscount short-term Treasury bills to an unlimited amount against banknotes. (The coverage requirement of one-third in gold, which still afforded a certain safeguard against inflation, was rendered illusory by the inclusion of the Loan Bank notes in the coverage, and later the gold-coverage requirements were legally repealed.)

Thus the financial war plan of the Government was as clear as it was simple and premeditated. The printing press had been chosen as the first resource for both the immediate war needs of the Reich and the increased credit requirements of private business. It was planned, in due time, to refund by a war loan the credits for which

The World War

the Reich had drawn upon the Reichsbank. But it was never contemplated to cover the war expenditures by means of taxation.

COSTS OF THE WORLD WAR

War expenditures rapidly grew to a point where they could be expressed only in astronomical figures. In the last fiscal year before the war (1913-14) Reich expenditures were 3,848,000,000 marks, to which must be added expenditures of the federal states of 8,507,000,-000 marks, a total of 12,355,000,000 marks. Compared with this, the expenditures of the Reich "occasioned by the war" reached the figures given in Table 8 (to which substantial expenditures by the federal states and the municipalities must be added).

TABLE 8

German War Expenditures

*Fiscal year
(ending March 31 of
the following year)*

1914	6,936,000,000
1915	23,909,000,000
1916	24,739,000,000
1917	42,188,000,000
1918	33,928,000,000
Carried forward from 1918	32,599,000,000
Total	164,300,000,000

German Economy

It should, of course, be taken into account that the purchasing power of the money declined considerably during the course of the war years. The simple summing up of the expenditures from year to year therefore does not give a true picture, based as it is on the fiction of "mark equal to mark." Thus the erratic increase in war expenditures from 1916 to 1917 and 1918 reflects, at least in some degree, the pronounced rise in prices. But if it were possible to find an exact formula by which all war expenditures could be reduced to prewar marks, one could probably still assess them well above 100,-000,000,000 prewar marks.

It has not yet become known to the public at large that at the beginning of the war Germany still hoped for some financial aid from abroad. A short, inconspicuous report by the Reich Debt Commission indicates that on August 8, 1914, the Reich Government printed Treasury certificates in the amount of $175,000,000, issued in United States dollars and inscribed in English, and sent them to the United States. This, after all, approximated 15 per cent of the first war-credit appropriations. In a later report the Reich Debt Commission drily remarks: "These Treasury certificates were never placed. They were canceled in the Imperial Embassy in Washington and will be returned to the Bureau of Control of State Securities (Kontrolle der Staatspapiere) as soon as traffic conditions permit sending them back from America."

The World War

Thus ended the first and most important attempt to procure war credits abroad. Similar attempts were repeated upon several later occasions. Their success has never been reported; it can have been only paltry. Anyhow, the fate of the Treasury certificates sent to America in 1914 makes it clear on which side the sympathies of the United States were from the very beginning, and how complete was Germany's isolation with respect to finance, as well as in other ways.

Thus Germany was wholly dependent on her domestic financial resources. Fortunately, the credit and currency system of modern economics is so elastic that it can cope with even the most extreme strains that may befall a country, provided only the authority of the Government remains intact. If the strain grows beyond a people's endurance, the final collapse need not necessarily come from the financial sphere. It may manifest itself as a purely physiological or psychological phenomenon in the political and social sphere, starting from the complete exhaustion of productive forces or of the human beings who have to operate them.

WAR LOANS AND BANK ADVANCES

As in all other belligerent nations, war loans were the most important means of financing the war in Germany. Their success was great beyond expectations, though it certainly was due in considerable degree to moral and

German Economy

political pressure on the public. Increasingly, and with little camouflage in the end, the war loans took on the character of forced loans.

Most of the war loans were issued in the form of 5 per cent loans without the obligation of repayment, but the Government had the right to call them at any time. Only a small part was issued in the form of 4½ per cent to 5 per cent Treasury certificates with various maturing terms. War loans were regularly issued at half-yearly intervals, nine times altogether. The results kept growing from the first to the eighth loan. The first war loan netted a nominal sum of 4,492,000,000 marks, the eighth, 15,126,000,000 marks, and only the last loan, issued a very short time before the collapse, showed a recession to 10,570,000,000 marks. In sum total, the Reich procured 96,929,000,000 marks from these loans, the total of the par value amounting to 99,265,000,000.

Although the sums flowing into the Treasury by way of war loans were enormous, still they did not cover more than 60 per cent of the war expenditures. To cover the rest only two "orthodox" methods were available: the more orthodox one, that of increased taxation, and the less orthodox, that of short-term credits extended by institutions other than the banks of issue. Actually the credit banks eagerly accepted the Treasury bills. The inflationary Reichsbank policy had greatly increased the "liquidity" of the banks, and an absolutely "secure," short-term, and rediscountable in-

The World War

vestment bearing interest at the rate of from 4½ per cent to 5 per cent seemed highly desirable. Thus the amount of Reich Treasury bills placed outside the Reichsbank increased to 29,300,000,000 marks by the end of the war.

WAR INFLATION

Since most of the war loans had the character of compulsory loans, it would have been tempting to save at least some of the great expenditure for interest payments by replacing the loans by taxes. Equally important psychological considerations would have prompted a drastic increase in taxation, to make some concession to the animosity of the public at large against the "war profiteers," the industrialists and tradesmen who enjoyed good business in the war boom.

Nevertheless, tax increases were resorted to only reluctantly and inefficiently. The Secretary of the Treasury, Karl Helfferich, before the war a director of the Deutsche Bank and the Anatolische Eisenbahngesellschaft, one of the most imposing figures among the civilians (nonmilitary persons) of the war regime, and one of the very few who continued to play an important role in Germany's political life after the war (until his tragic death in a railway accident in 1924), declared as late as March, 1915, in open Reichstag session that it was the intention of the Reich Government to finance the war exclusively by means of credits.

German Economy

Only very slowly, under the combined pressure from public opinion and the political parties, did the methods of financing change somewhat. War tax laws were adopted; the first batch came into force in June, 1916. They centered around two new taxes, a tax on war profits and a tax on turnover, at first with extremely low rates (one-tenth of 1 per cent on every subsequent turnover from producer to consumer). Both taxes were increased as the war went on, and other, chiefly indirect, taxes were added, of which the most important were a coal tax and a transportation tax.

The new taxes considerably increased the Reich's income. Net receipts, after deducting the expenditures of Reich enterprises, increased from 2,357,000,000 marks in 1914 to 7,830,000,000 in 1917, while there was a slight decrease during the fiscal year 1918. But this nominally important increase in Reich income was not even sufficient to balance the increase in ordinary Reich expenditure that resulted from the money depreciation and the increased interest burden for the war debt. The Reich expenditure, excluding direct war expenditure, amounted to 26,449,000,000 marks from 1914 to 1918 against an income of only 20,740,000,000 marks (not including the income from credits).

To explain the timidity of Germany's fiscal policy during the war it is usual to point primarily to the impediments implicit in her federal constitution. As has been described in the preceding chapter, the Reich was

106

The World War

endowed with very limited fiscal powers. The war, however, centralized the political power so tremendously that without any doubt the Reich could have wielded as much authority over fiscal policies as actually it did over industry.

If one adds as legal money coins in circulation, banknotes, Loan Bank notes, as well as the daily maturing liabilities of the Reichsbank, it may be stated that the circulation of state money increased during the war from 7,400,000,000 marks to 44,400,000,000, that is, to exactly six times the original amount. Private money, that is, deposits with the credit banks, increased somewhat less, from 4,900,000,000 marks to 19,100,000,000. But the total result is an increase in money circulation, public as well as private, from 12,500,000,000 marks to 63,500,000,000, that is, to five times the prewar amount.

The "German inflation" is usually thought of as a postwar phenomenon. The figures above indicate that the inflation began with the war, and that by its end it had exceeded any previous experience. At the end of the war Germany was, however, in such an extraordinary and unprecedented condition that the consequences of inflation on business were partly not realized, partly disguised by other factors.

During the entire war the German stock exchanges were closed, and quotations of foreign currencies were not published. Thus the consequences of inflation on the quotations of securities and foreign exchanges re-

107

German Economy

mained unknown to the public. The mark was, however, being quoted on the exchanges of the neutral countries, and there the effects of the German inflation could be gauged by the continually sinking value of the mark. At the end of the war the mark on the neutral exchanges had fallen to about half the gold parity.

The effects of inflation on domestic prices were likewise hidden by measures of war economy. The Statistical Reich Bureau computed after the war that the average level of German wholesale prices had increased 130 per cent during the war. But this computation took into account only the legal official maximum and normative prices, not the prices really paid. The more the "illicit trade" (*Schleichhandel*) at prices far above the official prices gained in momentum, the more these indices inevitably became fictitious. Only when the war economy with its all comprehensive restrictions had broken down did the real extent of the disturbances and dislocations become apparent.

2. WAR SOCIALISM

At the outbreak of the World War Germany was the greatest military land power in the world. But in one crucial respect, to become decisive after four years of struggle, she was at a disadvantage compared with the Allies: she was not master of the seas.

Germany was forced to form an "autarchic area" to-

108

The World War

gether with her own allies. Inside this sphere close market relations were formed, the German war industries exchanging their products for the (indeed very limited) surpluses of her allies in some raw materials and foodstuffs. These surpluses she was able to increase somewhat by conquest in southern and eastern Europe (Ukrainian grain, Rumanian oil); but throughout the war they remained much too small and few. Of course, trade was kept up to some extent with those neutral countries which were connected with Germany by a continental frontier, chiefly Holland, Switzerland, and Denmark. From all other countries Germany and her allies were shut off for all practical purposes, and British boats watched carefully to prevent goods from other countries from finding their way into Germany through neutral countries.

The blockade had qualitative and quantitative effects that were to prove fatal in the long run. The qualitative effect was that Germany had no access to certain raw materials she herself possessed either not at all or in insufficient quantities, which, however, were indispensable for implements of war, for example, certain metals, rubber, and oil. The quantitative effect of the blockade was that Germany was confined strictly to her own economic resources, from which she had to bolster up the even weaker resources of her allies by various economic and financial expedients, while the Allies not only could dispose of their own production, but in ad-

German Economy

dition had free access to the production of the whole world, and most important of all, to the immensely increasing production of the United States.

By cutting off Germany from all foreign resources the blockade must inevitably lead to her downfall—provided the war could be made to last long enough. But the end could be postponed if, as in a beleaguered fortress, a commandeered economy could be substituted for a free market economy. Thus the war imposed on Germany a complete change in her economic structure, and this new type of organization was to remain fundamental in the future.

When Germany entered the war, her economic life was intrinsically free, built on liberal, capitalistic principles, although much more interspersed with governmental regulations than in the Western countries. When the war ended, she had a thoroughly militarized economy, which, half in earnest, half ironically, was dubbed "War Socialism."

The shape of this economic organization was determined by dire necessity, not by a plan well thought out in advance. Thus business was not militarized with one stroke according to a plan, but, as the war dragged on, militarization gradually developed as scarcity appeared in one field after another.

For the scope of this study it may suffice to sketch the fundamental organizations in the three most im-

The World War

portant fields of war economy: the administration of food, of raw materials, and of labor relations.

FEEDING THE NATION

A highly industrialized country with a densely concentrated urban population like Germany is normally dependent on an exchange of domestic manufactured goods with the agricultural products of other countries. Before the war Germany produced no more than two-thirds of her food and fodder requirements, importing the other third. When a country living under such conditions as the war imposed on Germany is cut off from the importation of foodstuffs, it may for some time draw on the stocked-up reserves normally abundant in countries with a free economic system. This may be followed by all sorts of inducements to agriculture to increase production. But this will necessarily have only limited success when the men to till the soil are needed for war service, and the chemical plants have to turn out gunpowder instead of fertilizer.

The German War Food Administration indeed endeavored to use all the instruments available to an administration organized along military lines. It cut down consumption with ever increasing ruthlessness; it made new regulations for distribution, using new technical methods; besides, it experimented with all kinds of regulations of production. Even if the administration

German Economy

could have summoned the very best in planning wisdom, even if all the loopholes through which producers and consumers succeeded in escaping the net of regulations had been stopped, the physiological and psychological collapse after four and a half years of a hunger ordeal could not have been avoided. Food consumption was regulated in stages; the net was drawn closer and closer around the hapless consumer. Apart from lifting the agricultural tariffs and clamping down embargoes on foodstuffs, only a general law about maximum prices was passed at the beginning of the war. This empowered the authorities of the individual states to fix price limits on foodstuffs. It was not contemplated at that time to abolish the free food markets, but only to provide safeguards against any signs of panic. Only very gradually did maximum prices become more general, but as the war proceeded they at last covered almost every foodstuff throughout the country.

A maximum price system for foodstuffs without simultaneous regulation of consumption is like a "knife without handle and blade." At the moment of panic it may for a short time be efficient, but as a permanent system of distribution it must necessarily fail. It is not an effective method of guaranteeing equal distribution, which would be the main point, given an absolute scarcity of food.

The first attempt was to make the food scarcity more bearable by telling the consumer what to consume, or

The World War

better, what not to consume. As early as October, 1914, the notorious K-bread (war bread) was introduced by decreeing that the grain was not to be ground into flour beyond a prescribed percentage and that a fixed percentage of ersatz stuffs was to be mixed with the flour —potatoes at first, later even turnips or worse. It is up to the imagination of the reader to judge the quality of that kind of bread. A year later, two meatless days per week, on which meat should neither be marketed nor offered in public restaurants, were ordered.

Finally, an efficient instrument for regulating and curtailing consumption was found in the rationing system. The first card to be introduced was the bread card, January 25, 1915, by which the maximum amount of bread to be purchased for every member of a household was fixed. It was followed by cards for other essential foodstuffs (fats, meat, milk, butter, and so on). In the end an intricate system of consumption, differentiated according to physiological and social distinctions, had been built up. A flexible factor was introduced by fixing individual rations varying with the results of harvests and foreign resources. Of course, the trend was clearly downward. Physiological differentiations were made according to the character of the work demanded of the individual (preferences for "hard labor" and "hardest labor"), and partly according to age and other criteria; for example, children and expectant mothers were given preference in milk rations. In the last war

German Economy

years, milk (in tiny quantities) was distributed only to children and expectant mothers. The social differentiations consisted in constituting two preferred groups. The army was of course exempted from the entire card system; and the farmers as so-called self-providers were in theory allowed bigger rations than the rest of the population.

Under such a system naturally everything depends on the size of the rations. They varied in the course of the war years. But for an ordinary mortal who did not come under any one of the preferred categories the following rations may be taken as typical (although those were few and lucky who were actually able to get them): 225 grams of bread, or 200 grams of flour, per head daily, and 56 to 68 grams of fatstuffs (butter, lard, or margarine) per head weekly. Vegetables (except potatoes) and fruit were usually available in more or less sufficient quantities, but in all other foodstuffs there was dire shortage, which could in no way be alleviated by the abundant crop of the ersatz industries.

Agricultural production, too, was subjected to a system of compulsory regulations, which remained ineffective as far as they were supposed to compel farmers to increase their production, or were very questionable in their effects as far as they tended to deflect production into certain channels.

As an illustration, the famous story of the "hog massacre" may be cited. (In later years it loomed large in the

The World War

propaganda of the rising Nazi tide.) It began with the authorities nursing the belief that the hog was to be considered as a competitor of man for the limited food supplies. They figured out exactly how much grain and potatoes hogs "ate away" from man, and then proclaimed the class war of the starving humans against the greedy pigs. The underlying theory was that the detour of foodstuffs over the stomach of the pigs was uneconomic from the standpoint of rational nutrition when only a limited total of foodstuffs was available. But this theory did not lead them to the most rational way of altering the proportionate supply of grain and potatoes on the one hand and hogs on the other, which would have been so to regulate maximum prices as to provide the farmer with a greater incentive to sell his grain and potatoes than to feed them to the hogs. Instead, the way of compulsion was chosen. In the autumn of 1914 an embargo was put on using wheat and rye as fodder for animals; the quantities of oats and barley allowed for feeding purposes were rationed. Finally, in the beginning of 1915, for fear lest these regulations would not be strictly observed and that an acute potato shortage was in the offing—which would have hit one of the most important foodstuffs of the German masses—all municipalities were forced by decree to stock up certain reserves of packed meat. This gave the signal for the "hog massacre." After the forced slaughtering of hogs had continued for some time, it was found that the potato

German Economy

supply had been underrated, and now the opposite danger arose: that there would be an insufficient number of pigs to eat the potatoes. Accordingly, criticism of this "St. Bartholomew's Day of the bristle-bearers" became vocal.

Yet the disturbance in the popular food supply consequent upon the forced hog slaughter was a relatively minor incident, and the story is of value merely as a significant example of the sort of error to which every planning system is probably exposed.

The system of compulsory regulation of farm production was extended further and further. But none of these measures could succeed in stopping the decay of agriculture that resulted from the deficiency in farm hands, fertilizer, and implements. At the end of the war, not only had the livestock on German farms run down to an alarming low, but grain production also had decreased to less than half of the yields of prewar years, as far as could be ascertained officially. Together with the rest of Germany, agriculture was at the end of its tether.

COMPULSORY REGULATION OF INDUSTRY

To a large extent modern war has become a matter of industrial capacity. Under normal conditions the food needs of an army at war are not considerably in excess of what the standing army and the reservists called to service need before mobilization. But what is

The World War

measurably increased from the very outset of a war is the demand for special industrial products. Accordingly, the seriousness of Germany's emergency was recognized much earlier in the industrial field than in agriculture, and compulsory measures were taken during the first two weeks

It is the historical merit of Walter Rathenau—later the great Foreign Minister of the Weimar Germany, but in 1914 head of the General Electric Company founded by his father Emil—that he was the first to realize the emergency and to act with initiative and energy. In order to appreciate what boldness Rathenau, a mere private citizen, although a captain of industry, needed to enter the holy precincts of the War Ministry and lay before the leaders of the nation's destiny a plan for the management of the country's raw-material supplies, one must recall with what tremendous weight the military hierarchy of prewar Germany reigned over public life. The impression created by this plan was so deep that in August, 1914, the Prussian War Minister immediately appointed Walter Rathenau chief of the War Raw Material Office (Kriegs-Rohstoffabteilung, K.R.A.), formed according to his own plan. In this capacity, Rathenau laid the foundations for the German War Industry Administration.

The so-called war companies (*Kriegsgesellschaften*) founded on Rathenau's initiative had a certain kinship to the mixed-ownership companies developed prior to

German Economy

the war. In the war companies elements of private and of public ownership formed a peculiar mixture, in respect to both their legal setup and the powers in control. Usually private stock or limited-liability companies were organized, which, however, differed from genuine private companies in the public functions assigned to them: to administer sequestrated raw materials, and to act as trustees for the Government. In fact, the companies were controlled jointly by the Government and the original owners, producers, or processors of these raw materials. As far as they remained under the control of private industrialists, they were autonomous organs of industry under government control and for public purposes.

Necessarily, these war companies degenerated rapidly. On the one hand, they were blamed for allegedly permitting excessive war profits to the industries connected with them, and it is true that they could not prevent profits from being made, although it was one of their tasks to keep profits of their member companies within bounds. On the other hand, the basic principle of self-government was certain to be more and more curtailed with the growing scarcity in raw materials, and thereby the war companies were transformed into purely bureaucratic agencies.

Even so, Rathenau's creative idea of these war companies became one of the important directives for the subsequent development of German state economy. All

The World War

subsequent efforts of Weimar Germany and, ironically enough, of the Third Reich to develop state economy on nonbureaucratic lines and to create intermediary institutions between private and public business management are to be traced back to Rathenau's organizing genius.

In the first war years the Government confined its measures to the industrial sphere: (1) sequestrating raw materials as they began to get scarce by decreeing that the producers had to sell them to the war companies; (2) fixing maximum prices; (3) reselling the raw materials to the processor for limited uses. Distribution to manufacturers was according to the "urgency" of their production.

The shift toward complete "War Socialism" in the so-called Hindenburg program did not occur until the end of 1916. Together with the unrestricted U-boat war, this was to be the nation's supreme effort. By mustering all economic forces Germany tried to break through the strategy of exhaustion applied by her enemies, and to force ultimate victory.

The Hindenburg Program was legally enacted by the law of December 5, 1916, on Patriotic Auxiliary Service (*Vaterländischer Hilfsdienst*). It was planned to complete the militarization of the economic life of the nation. The law provided that every male German citizen from seventeen to sixty years of age not in active military service was to be regarded as a member of the

German Economy

Auxiliary Service. Actually the law was made applicable principally to workers in the workshops directly or indirectly employed in war industries or on farms, who were deprived of their freedom of movement. They could not change their employment without the approval of the employer or of a committee. If these workshops had difficulties in procuring the necessary hands by voluntary methods, workers could be conscripted.

The compulsory service of the workshops themselves consisted in the drafting of their production for munition supplies. Plants not adapted to this kind of production would be deprived of their workers and thus forced to shut down or to amalgamate with other companies. State control over private industrial companies went so far that unused machinery could be drafted and allotted to other workshops. Finally, the law provided for the retraining of workers for munition work.

3. SOCIAL CHANGES

In a previous chapter we showed how much power the German trade-unions had achieved before the war and how closely they were woven into the texture of German economic life. But prior to 1914 this important factor of German social organization had lacked a clear legal status. Officially, the Free Unions were still considered as revolutionary and therefore illegitimate, al-

The World War

though after the repeal of the Anti-Socialist Laws no longer as illegal associations. But the Social-Democratic party, with which they were connected, still pretended to be a revolutionary opposition party, even when, under the leadership of Bebel and Wilhelm Liebknecht, it had grown into the largest German party.

By voting for the war credits the Social-Democrats abandoned this pretense, as also happened in the western and northern countries of Europe. Before August 4, 1914, the Social-Democratic party was officially a revolutionary party, but actually a party of loyal opposition. After that date it was officially a loyal opposition party, but actually a government party with only those evident limitations which the Bismarckian system of government imposed on all government parties. They were allowed to vote for the Government, but they were not themselves called to form the Government and the administration.

This change was, of course, bound to have its influence on the status of the unions, particularly since at the same time the industrial war requirements tended to enhance their power automatically. In their relations with the employers the unions, however, did not press this advantage openly. On August 4 on the political field practically a National Government front, which included all parties, was formed (the Independent Social-Democrats were to secede from the mother party only at a later stage of the war). At the same time,

121

German Economy

August 2, on the economic field a "truce" (*Burgfrieden*) was concluded, an expression that goes back to the medieval knights. As all personal feuds among the defenders in a beleaguered fortress are suspended until the enemy is repulsed, the German unions and employers agreed to suspend all labor strife for the duration of the war.

A natural consequence of the shortage of labor was that the real power of the unions was not hampered in any way by this official renunciation of the strike weapon. And later upon some critical occasions it became evident that the organized workers themselves, if not the unions as such, knew very well how to handle this weapon.

THE WELFARE POLICY IN WARTIME

The war brought the beginnings of unemployment relief in Germany. As early as August 4, 1914, without any connection with unemployment relief, payments were promised to destitute families of soldiers in war service. At that time it was still seriously believed that the war would cause permanent mass unemployment. A little later, several municipalities began on their own account to dole out relief to their unemployed, and after December, 1914, the Reich itself provided the municipalities with funds for unemployment relief. The

The World War

dole was given only after proof of genuine need, a system that remained in force until 1926.

Not all industries profited by the "war boom." It is self-evident that in general consumer goods were much less in demand than raw materials and durable goods. And among consumer-goods industries the textile industries were foremost among those the "war boom" passed by, chiefly because of lack of raw materials. Despite the draft for war service, there was unemployment in the textile industries, and textile wages were least adjusted to the rising cost of living.

Thus it came about that the textile industries were the first to develop the new principles of social reform that later in Weimar Germany were to become fundamentally important. The Government intervened by assuming responsibility not only for procuring employment but also for distributing the available opportunities among the workers as fairly as possible. The employers were allowed to discharge workers only in exceptional cases, and in order to spread labor, working hours in the textile industries were shortened by decree. On August 12, 1915, the Federal Council (Bundesrat) cut down work in spinning and weaving plants to at most five days a week, a 10-hour working day at that time still being the rule. Finally on November 18, 1915, a general textile workers' dole was decreed, to be paid to needy textile workers even when at work.

German Economy

MEDIATION COMMISSIONS AND SHOP COMMITTEES

Despite maximum-price legislation and compulsory management of material resources, the war years were a period of rising prices. As this trend originated not in rising wages but in monetary measures, wages tended to lag behind prices. In an endeavor to stop this source of social unrest the military authorities began to take some interest in employer-employee relations. They not only favored but also initiated negotiations between the unions and employers. Often they went so far as to set minimum wages as a condition for the award of military orders. Finally, in some places the military authorities instituted conciliation committees on which employers and employees were equally represented.

But the decisive step was taken upon the occasion of the Hindenburg Program, when workers' committees and conciliation committees were formed. The workers' committees were the outcome of a compromise between the Government and the Social-Democratic party (and the trade-unions). The Social-Democrats declared themselves willing to assent to the complete militarization of the factory workers asked for by the Hindenburg Program only on condition that the workers' interests were to be safeguarded by workers' councils.

Accordingly, the Law on Patriotic Auxiliary Service (*Gesetz über den vaterländischen Hilfsdienst*) set up

The World War

workers' committees. In every plant with fifty or more workers these committees were formed by secret ballot among the employees, by proportional representation. The workers' committees were the immediate precursors of the shop-council system inaugurated by the Weimar Constitution, which was to become one of the most important features of the new labor system. The Auxiliary Service Law provided also for conciliation committees formed of an equal number of representatives of employers and employees under the chairmanship of an official conciliator. They were to decide on all wage problems, and their decisions were binding.

4. THE END

In the bitter struggle between Republican Germany and her foes from the Right, which ended with the destruction of the Republic, the so-called stab-in-the-back legend always played an important role. The parties of the Right contended that Germany's defeat was not a military defeat, but was caused by a stab in the back administered to the fighting army by the "hinterland" (the people at home).

The military history of the World War admits of no doubt as to which side commanded the superior forces in the last phase of the war. Slowly but surely, at the front as well as in the hinterland, the ultimate limits in the exploitation of all German resources came in sight.

German Economy

In technical equipment the German Army was surpassed more and more by the Allied armies; the scales were weighted more and more to the advantage of that group of powers whose resources, superior to those of the Central Powers from the start, were at last rendered practically limitless by the accession of the new American ally, the greatest industrial power of the world.

There is, however, no doubt that among the factors decisive in the end for the relation of forces on both sides of the trenches there were quite a number of subtle moral factors, among which the morale of the army and of the hinterland were paramount. It is not hard to visualize what must have been the state of morale of a nation from which for four years the most terrific sacrifices of life and limb and wealth had been exacted, which more and more felt doomed to starvation, and at last was forced to realize that its last military card, unrestrained submarine war, was not trumps, but on the contrary had brought the new and unexhausted armies of the greatest country of Western civilization into the enemy camp.

These moral factors worked just as well on the fronts as in the hinterland. They could not therefore constitute a stab in the back of the fronts. The only difference between hinterland and front was that the effects of moral disintegration were more visible in the hinterland, where men were not subjected to quite the same degree of military discipline as in the trenches. In the economic

126

The World War

sphere the most telling symptoms of this disintegration were the illicit trade and the strikes.

Even the most energetic government actions were powerless in the face of illicit trade spreading to commodities whose distribution was officially regulated. This not only weakened public morale by accustoming people to infringements of the law. It also enhanced the differences between rich and poor, and thus hastened the decomposition of the public spirit. Nothing is more conducive to the belief that a war is only "a war for the rich," and nothing accordingly is more disruptive of morale, than a condition that makes the upper classes appear unwilling to shoulder the burdens along with the lower strata of society. The spreading of illicit trade proved clearly that the upper classes were no longer possessed of the moral force to bear their share of the sacrifices imposed on the nation as a whole. The decline of war morale did not originate among the lower classes alone.

For the strike wave, the other symptom of disintegration, there was undoubtedly at least in part some causal connection with the Russian Revolution, which began in the spring of 1917 with the downfall of Czarism and culminated in the Bolshevik November Revolution. Some time before these events, a group openly opposed to the war had been formed in Germany; in 1916 the Independent Social-Democratic party broke away from the Social-Democratic party. But although a wave of

German Economy

excitement spread over Germany after the outbreak of the Russian Revolution in 1917, and various opposition groups began partly legal, partly illegal activities, none of the large strikes of the last war years was genuinely revolutionary in character. The strikes were almost exclusively caused by the distressing food shortage, although, of course, the propaganda of revolutionary Socialist groups contributed to their spread.

On April 16, 1917—that is, immediately after the collapse of Czarism in Russia—the Reich Government cut down bread rations. This caused such excitement among the working population that in numerous munition factories, particularly in the great cities and in the Ruhr district, spontaneous strikes ensued. After negotiations between the Government and the central bodies of the trade-unions and the Social-Democratic party, the bread rations were restored until such time as sufficient ersatz for bread could be offered. This ended the strike wave, but from time to time strikes flared up again. In January, 1918, a widespread strike move harried the munitions industries, but this also was of short duration.

In July, 1918, an unauthorized strike began in the Upper Silesian mining industry, with an objective reflecting the state of food supplies in Germany. The striking workers demanded that daily working hours be cut to eight, since, owing to the inadequate food, their physical strength was not up to working longer hours. Note, however, that workers classified as "hardest

The World War

workers" were awarded the highest rations. The military authorities countered the strike by proclaiming a "major state of siege" and by putting all mine workers of this district under military law. But in August, 1918, while the strike was at its height, the altered situation on the war fronts brought to a sudden halt the dictatorship of the Supreme Army Command. In October, 1918, the Reichstag, which now in fact took over the Government, accepted a constitutional amendment by which the power of the military authorities to proclaim martial law was strictly limited. A few days later the Supreme Army Command appealed to the Government to take up peace negotiations at once, because the front was on the point of breaking up.

This narrative shows two things: first, that the almost superhuman sacrifices imposed on the German people in overstraining all the economic and military forces of the nation had slowly but surely undermined its power of resistance; second, that the final collapse was caused by military, economic, and physiological processes, not by political factors. The "stab in the back" is merely a legend. The flames kindled by the Russian Revolution surely enhanced the readiness of the German workers to make use of the strike weapon. But the strikes themselves, indicative as they were of fading of powers of resistance, were not important and persistent enough in themselves to constitute a decisive cause of the sudden and surprising breakdown.

German Economy

At the moment of Germany's military collapse, the economic and psychological forces, too, were just on the brink of complete exhaustion. The military collapse became unavoidable when the Allies were accorded the fresh resources of their great American ally just at the time when all German war activities were becoming more and more crippled by lack of munitions. On the other hand, the hopelessness of the military situation, which in spite of censorship at last became a matter of common knowledge in Germany, precipitated the breakdown of German morale.

PART IV

THE WEIMAR REPUBLIC

THE WEIMAR REPUBLIC

I. GENERAL CHARACTERIZATION

THE REVOLUTION that followed the military collapse brought a fundamental change in Germany's political structure. The economic changes were much less revolutionary once several timid attempts at nationalization of the key industries had failed.

It is true that the economic structure of the Germany of 1932 was very different from that of 1914. In itself this economic structure would have been ripe for a Socialist regime. The tendency to let all economic relations be "penetrated by the state" (*Durchstaatlichung*) by no means originated in the revolution of 1918. The revolution merely accentuated an evolution that, apart from the relatively short period of early Bismarckian liberalism, seems traditional in German history. This trend had kept growing in the last decades before the war and at last became dominant during and because of the war.

The German Republic had a brief but adventurous life. From both a political and an economic point of view we may distinguish three well-defined periods in the short span of fourteen years.

The first lasted five years, from November, 1918, to

133

German Economy

November, 1923. Politically it was the period of the worst disorders and of dangerous attempts on the life of the young Republic, while economically it was dominated by the inflation. The era of political unrest, of Putsches, and of political murder came to an end on the very same day as the inflation. On November 9, 1923, the musical-comedy Putsch of Hitler and Ludendorff in Munich was defeated. On November 15, 1923, the currency was stabilized.

The second period lasted until the end of 1929. It was terminated by the death of Gustav Stresemann, the last Foreign Minister of the Republic to enjoy both national and international confidence and authority. Stresemann died in October, 1929, about the time of the collapse of the great American boom. Politically and economically, this was the time of the flowering of the Weimar Republic. German democracy had apparently been consolidated, and this political stabilization was accompanied by an economic boom on a truly American scale.

The third phase, which lasted to the end of 1932, was the industrial, agricultural, and banking crisis. Like the boom period, it can be measured only by American standards. There was only one difference between Germany and America, but it was fundamental. America's democracy was established beyond any doubt. The economic crisis therefore could do nothing worse than bring about the traditional exchange of places between

The Weimar Republic

the ruling party and the opposition. The young German democracy, on the contrary, was not yet consolidated enough to survive the shock of the crisis.

We now propose to describe the three periods separately and then show their common traits.

2. INFLATION, 1918-1923

THE VERSAILLES TREATY

On entering the Weimar period of inflation and then of reconstruction, Germany as a territorial unit was very different from the powerful nation of the last prewar years. Not only had she lost all her colonies, whose value, as we have seen, was problematical, but also the Reich proper (counting among the lost provinces the Saar region, which remained separated from Germany up to 1935) had lost 13.1 per cent of its prewar territory and 10 per cent of the population of 1910. The territories lost permanently or until 1935 in consequence of the Versailles Treaty and the partition of Upper Silesia (1921) were particularly rich in agricultural and mineral resources. They comprised 14.6 per cent of the arable area of Germany, 74.5 per cent of German iron ore, 68.1 per cent of her zinc ore, 26 per cent of her coal production. Add to this the disruption of the German potash monopoly (by the loss of the Alsatian potash mines) and the transformation of the

German Economy

Alsatian textile industries from one of the most powerful factors of the prosperous German textile industries into their most dangerous competitors. Finally, it should not be overlooked that the loss of Alsace-Lorraine, and even more the partition of Upper Silesia, destroyed some of the most important interconnections of the industrial and transportation systems.

In other words, the loss of territory made Germany considerably poorer than she had been. And this loss was immensely increased by the deliveries in kind imposed on Germany by the Armistice and the peace treaty. In addition to the armament material, including the entire navy, Germany had to deliver:

All merchant ships exceeding 1,600 gross tons
Half of the merchant ships between 1,000 and 1,600 gross tons
One-quarter of the fishing fleet
One-fifth of the river and lake fleet
Five thousand locomotives, 150,000 railway cars, 5,000 motor trucks
The entire Alsace-Lorraine railway system, with all rolling stock
All material relinquished in the war zone
All public property in the ceded territories and in the colonies

Furthermore, the Allies reserved the right to confiscate all German private property in their own countries and in the ceded territories. (The German citizens were to be compensated by the Reich Government.) This threat was subsequently made good, except in the

The Weimar Republic

ceded territories. The United States alone set a notable exception by later returning the sequestrated private property.

The crediting of all these deliveries to the reparation account—at wholly arbitrary valuations—was purely fictitious. In view of the astronomical size of the reparation totals, this crediting was like pouring wine into a barrel without bottom.

These deliveries and losses of territory resulted in a catastrophic deterioration of the German balance of payments. Larger food imports became necessary; minerals until then mined in Germany had to be bought abroad, the exports of others had to be reduced. The loss of her merchant fleet deprived Germany of income from transportation paid by foreign countries. The loss of her capital investments abroad meant the loss of profits and interest previously received from these countries. Even without reparation payments, it would therefore have been very hard for Germany to regain a balance in her foreign exchanges, unless she were accorded foreign help.

REPARATIONS

The reparations rendered the German situation definitely hopeless for the next few years. When on October 3, 1918, Prince Max von Baden's government accepted Wilson's Fourteen Points, it thereby accepted

German Economy

also the obligation to repair the devastated war zones. The note sent by Secretary of State Lansing to the German Government on November 5, 1918, defined this reparation obligation more precisely. Germany was to undertake to repair the damages to private property, except that of Russia.[1] Had the computation of these damages been fair, the obligations would probably have been balanced to a large extent by the deliveries enumerated above. But the reparations as ultimately defined had lost their relation to the original American definition.

The Versailles Treaty first obligated Germany to pay all costs of Allied occupation troops on German territory, this being a superimposed obligation not credited to the reparation account; second, it extended the reparations to include all (capitalized) pensions for Allied combatants, swelling the reparation figures enormously. A total sum for the reparation obligations was however not set by the peace treaty, which provided only that the German Government was to issue and deliver at once bonds to the amount of 100,000,000,000 gold marks, of which 20,000,000,000 were to serve as security for the interim payments up to May 1, 1921. Interest and amortization on the rest were to be paid during the thirty subsequent years. This alone implied

[1] Literally: "Compensation will be made by Germany for all damage done to the *civilian* population of the Allies and to their property by the aggression of Germany by land, sea, and from the air."

138

The Weimar Republic

an annual reparation payment of 1,000,000,000 gold marks after 1921. To the Reparation Commission provided for by the peace treaty was assigned the task of deciding on the definite amount and the mode of payment of the reparations total. The plan was to be completed by May 1, 1921.

Although the peace treaty did not come into force until January 10, 1920, it called for German payments of 20,000,000,000 gold marks before May 1, 1921, against which the deliveries provided by it (delivery of the merchant fleet, and so on) were to be credited. Part of the rest of this amount was to be paid by "deliveries in kind" (*Sachlieferungen*). On this count Germany was obligated to deliver over a decade at least 38,000,000 tons of coal a year, and huge quantities of chemicals and other commodities. The deliveries in kind began in fact in August, 1919; that is, before the peace treaty came into force.

The following years up to the time of the Dawes Plan (1924) were filled with bitter and pernicious struggles over the amount and the mode of reparation payments. At last in January, 1921, a plan of payments was resolved upon (the Paris Resolutions), which provided for the payment of 2,000,000,000 gold marks each in the first two years, 3,000,000,000 each in the following three years, 4,000,000,000 again for three more years, 5,000,000,000 for the following three years, 6,000,000,000 for the next thirty-one years, and in ad-

German Economy

dition 26 per cent of the proceeds from German exports in each of these forty-two years. As the reparation payments in themselves forced Germany to fantastically huge exports, the 26 per cent export duty constituted an additional reparation burden that would rapidly rise to from 2,000,000,000 to 3,000,000,000 per annum.

Already at that time the Allies tried to make the German Government accept this absurd plan by imposing "sanctions," as provided by the peace treaty. In March, 1921, several towns on the Rhine and in the Ruhr Basin were occupied, and the customs receipts in the occupied territories were impounded.

The "final" plan of payments elaborated by the Reparation Commission in April, 1921, and presented to Germany by the Allied governments in the first days of May, the so-called London Ultimatum, was hardly closer to reality than the Paris Resolutions. First, Germany's reparation debt was fixed at 132,000,000,000 gold marks, an amount, which according to the most eminent economic expert on the Allied side, J. M. Keynes, exceeded by three times the German ability to pay.[2] The reparation debt was to bear 6 per cent annually in interest and amortization. But at first the Reparation Commission was to issue only 50,000,000,000 gold-mark bonds to be serviced by the reparation payments. The

[2] Keynes proposed to put the reparation obligations at 42,000,000,000 gold marks, of which 11,000,000,000 should be regarded as offset by the delivery of the ships. The balance would be paid in thirty annuities of 1,050,000,000 marks.

140

The Weimar Republic

rest, 82,000,000,000 marks, was not to be issued until the commission was satisfied that Germany was able to bear the additional burden.

At first the reparation annuities were fixed at 2,000,-000,000 plus the 26 per cent export duty, a sum virtually identical with the one provided by the Paris Resolutions for the first years. As down payment Germany was to deliver 1,000,000,000 gold marks in cash within the next few months. The full German export duties plus the special 26 per cent export duty plus several tax receipts were to serve as guarantee for these payments. A guarantee committee sitting in Berlin was to watch over the execution of this plan. The Reparation Commission was given the right to demand "payment in kind" for any part of the reparations. The German Government was further requested to let the British Government take charge of cashing in its part of the 26 per cent export duty (British Recovery Act), while the German Government was to compensate the German exporters.

This reparation plan was presented to Germany in the form of an ultimatum. Should the German Government not accept within six days, the Ruhr Basin would be occupied. The German Reichstag accepted, by a bare majority. In the following months the plan was actually executed in the time limits fixed, and even the 1,000,000,000 marks in cash was paid before the end of August, 1921. Not until December did the German Government ask for a reduction. In January, 1922, it

German Economy

was agreed that the payments for 1922 were to be reduced to 2,170,000,000 marks and the additional payments for the armies of occupation canceled. Of the total, not more than 720,000,000 marks were to be paid in cash, the rest in kind. This agreement was executed up to July, 1922. Meanwhile Germany's situation had deteriorated to such a degree that the Government begged for a moratorium on cash payments up to the end of 1924, declaring itself willing to keep up deliveries in kind to the agreed maximum of 1,450,000,000 marks. The moratorium was not granted, but in September, 1922, it was agreed that besides the deliveries in kind the Reich Government was to pay 270,000,000 marks in six-month Treasury certificates.

THE RUHR STRUGGLE

Thus the reparation payments had largely been converted into deliveries in kind, and it was on this field that the hard reparation struggle of 1923 was carried on. The Poincaré government in power in France was convinced that Germany was evading her obligations in bad faith, and that there was no other way of retrieving reparations than to go and get them. The method was to occupy the Ruhr Basin, the center of Germany's coal and iron production. A minor conflict between Germany and France, or more correctly between Germany and the Reparation Commission, had arisen over the

The Weimar Republic

delivery of telegraph poles and a small deficiency in coal deliveries. This was taken as a pretext by France and Belgium to march into the Ruhr in January, 1923.

Now for the first time Germany revolted openly against a measure taken by the victorious powers. At the moment the French and Belgian armies marched into the Ruhr, the German Government stopped all reparation payments to France and Belgium, and prohibited all German officials, including the Reichsbahn officials, from taking orders from the occupying authorities. The latter responded by evicting all German officials from the Ruhr, by organizing a civil and railroad administration of their own, by cutting off the Ruhr economically from the rest of Germany, and by sequestrating the funds of banks and Reichsbank branches in the Ruhr and stocks in factories and mines. After passive resistance, first ordered for officials, had spread to the workers in mines and industries, the occupying authorities tried, by force, to keep up activity in the workshops, partly with the aid of their own men.

The Ruhr struggle plunged Germany into the direst straits. She was now separated from her most important industrial raw-material resources. Moreover, the Government had to feed the workers and officials who had struck in, or who had been evicted from, the Ruhr territory, to maintain the families of thousands who were thrown into jail by the enemy, and on top of it all, to

143

German Economy

compensate industry heavily for the losses suffered in the conflict. Nevertheless, the deliveries in kind to the Allies, except those to France and Belgium, were maintained until August, 1923, as were the payments provided by the British Recovery Act. Add to this plight the rising political chaos in consequence of the complete collapse of the currency, and the ultimate crumbling of resistance seems only too natural. In August, 1923, the Cuno government, which had carried on the Ruhr struggle, resigned. The new coalition government, headed by Dr. Gustav Stresemann, at once stopped the passive-resistance movement and the payments to resisting workers and officials. In November, 1923, agreements were arrived at between the occupation authorities and representatives of the industrialists, with the concurrence of the German Government, according to which the companies were to pay taxes and deliver commodities directly to the Allies. These agreements remained in force until the Dawes Plan was accepted in August, 1924.

Thus, certainly not by pure chance, the end of the Ruhr struggle coincided with the end of the inflation. The situation called for a complete reconstruction of German finances and currency on the one hand, and of the relations between Germany and the Allies on the other, neither of which could be accomplished without the other.

The Weimar Republic

FINANCIAL REFORMS

Despite all these handicaps, prior to the Dawes Plan immense efforts had been made from time to time to get rid of the budget deficit, which threatened to grow out of all bounds, overburdened as the budget was with reparations, the interest service for the gigantic war loans, and the relief for war victims. Even before the fundamental financial reforms of 1920 several taxes (chiefly the turnover tax) were increased, and export duties were put into force. In December, 1919, the Reich Emergency Levy (*Reichsnotopfer*) was voted by the Reichstag, a capital levy that was to take as much as 65 per cent of the largest properties, while also reaching down to the smallest properties, and to net not less than 80,000,000,000 marks, a sum equal to more than 8,000,000,000 prewar marks in purchasing power at the time the bill was passed. But soon there was to appear the intrinsic weakness of a financial policy that in a period of progressive depreciation of the currency defined the taxes in terms of nominal money values. As delays up to several years must intervene between the assessment of a tax and its payment, the tax proceeds would shrink to a fraction of the expected amount if the currency had meanwhile depreciated. For the Reich Emergency Levy this weakness was especially marked, because long-drawn-out installment payments had to be granted. The purchasing power of the installments did

145

German Economy

not vary much in 1920, but began to decline in 1921, and continued at such a rate that soon it was no longer worth while to enforce payment. In 1922 installments on the levy were suspended, and replaced by a current property tax.

The most ambitious and systematic attempt to solve the financial problems was undertaken through Erzberger's tax reforms. The importance of these reforms far transcended the mere balancing of the budget. They made a vivid reality of the constitutional innovations the Weimar Constitution had provided in the field of public finance: the transformation of Germany from a federalistic group of states into a centralized state. As pointed out in the preceding chapter, in Bismarck's Germany the Reich could avail itself of only the few sources of taxation not claimed by the states. Now the Reich was made the supreme bearer of financial sovereignty, and the states were limited to those taxes not claimed by the Reich.

What was established as a theoretical proposition by the Weimar Constitution was made effective by Erzberger's financial reforms. Despite the confusion of the inflation period, these reforms created a system of Reich taxes which, with relatively few changes, has remained up to the present the foundation of Germany's fiscal system. At the same time the Reich organized a well-devised fiscal administration, the first comprehensive nonmilitary executive organization ever set up by the

The Weimar Republic

Reich, which otherwise was dependent on the executive organs and thereby on the co-operative goodwill of the states.

Incidentally, Matthias Erzberger had eminent achievements to his credit, not only as Minister of Finance but also in many other fields. They made him one of the great political figures of the war and postwar years. During the war, as a leader of the Center party, he was the strongest force behind the peace endeavors of the later "Weimar parties," and especially behind the Reichstag's peace resolution of July, 1917. As one of the most prominent representatives of the new Germany he was the target of all attacks from the Right, particularly when he attempted a rigid taxation of property. Nevertheless he continued to pursue this course until he was forced by a campaign of calumnies to resign from his post as Finance Minister. Finally, in August, 1921, he became the victim of a National Socialist attempt on his life. His end was similar to that of another great leader of the young Republic, Walter Rathenau. After his accession to power Hitler honored the murderers of both by the dedication of public monuments.

Well-planned and efficient as Erzberger's reforms proved to be after the inflation, they had to fail, just as all previous financial measures had failed, overwhelmed by the progressive deterioration of the currency. Therefore in 1922, when the tempo of depreciation had become faster, the political battle for another capital levy on a

German Economy

large scale was once more renewed. To stop the inflation, the Socialist parties demanded a large capital levy, the idea being that this tax could be made effective by tapping so-called physical values *(Sachwerte)*. This rather nebulous expression was understood at that time to comprise all property titles not immediately affected by the inflation, such as factories, commodity stocks, and real estate. The "bourgeois" parties opposed this proposal as leading to a partial socialization of business under a fiscal pretense without the hope of solving the financial problems finally. The "compromise" eventually arrived at provided for a compulsory loan of 1,000,000,000 gold marks bearing no interest for the first three years, then from 4 per cent to 5 per cent. Although this loan was made out in "gold marks," by which the fictitious formula of "mark equal to mark" was for the first time officially abandoned, still, between the time of assessment and collection the receipts depreciated at such a rate that the whole scheme remained largely on paper.

Thus the results of all financial struggles and experiments during the entire period of inflation were largely negative. In spite of tax increases, the Reich Emergency Levy, and the compulsory loan, tax receipts dropped off to hopeless depths after the depreciation of the currency had taken a catastrophic turn.

If one defines as "purchasing-power mark" the paper mark divided by the cost-of-living index on a given

The Weimar Republic

date, the relation of Reich income and expenditures during the inflation period is expressed by the figures in Table 9.

TABLE 9

Reich Finance 1920-1923
("purchasing-power marks")

April 1 to March 31	Income	Expenditures	Excess of expenditures over income
1920–1921 ...	4,091,000,000	11,266,000,000	7,175,000,000
1921–1922 ...	5,236,000,000	11,964,000,000	6,728,000,000
1922–1923 ...	3,529,000,000	9,665,000,000	6,136,000,000
1923–1924 ...	1,245,000,000	12,977,000,000	11,732,000,000

The deficit was covered by "floating debts," that is to say, by the printing press. Table 9 shows clearly that the decisive turn for the worse in both income and expenditures occurred in 1923. This was the price Germany had to pay for the Ruhr struggle.

THE WHIRL OF THE DEVISEN

From May, 1919, when the peace conditions became known, until February, 1920, the dollar quotation (parity at 4.20 marks) moved from 13.5 up to 99 marks. This period was characterized on the one hand by the shock following the announcement of the peace-treaty terms, on the other hand by the domestic troubles that in March, 1920, culminated in the Kapp Putsch. After this had been put down in the same month, the dollar

German Economy

rapidly dropped to 40 marks (June, 1920) and oscillated between 60 and 70 marks for an entire year. It was a period of domestic appeasement characterized by the first deflationary effects of Erzberger's reforms and by a breathing spell in the reparation struggle. The London Ultimatum of May, 1921, and the partition of Upper Silesia in October of the same year, which together plunged the German nation into a deep depression, sent the dollar up to 270 marks (November, 1921). A short period of receding Devisen (foreign-exchange) quotations followed when the German Government was granted a partial moratorium on reparation payments. But after June, 1922, the foreign-exchange quotations resumed their upward movement following large cash payments on reparations, and the assassination of Rathenau, which was indicative of the growing domestic tension. In July, 1922, the mark for the first time sank to less than 1 per cent of its peacetime value, and when Poincaré's reparation policy was seen to be preparing for the Ruhr occupation, the plunge became ruinous. By January, 1923, when the Ruhr adventure had started, the dollar quotation reached 18,000 marks. Then, surprisingly enough, the exchange market quieted down somewhat. One of Germany's maneuvers in the Ruhr struggle was to defend the currency by all possible means. But after May, 1923, the economic consequences of the Ruhr resistance for German finance and business became so catastrophic that the support of the mark had to be abandoned, and

The Weimar Republic

the quotations broke once more. From then on nothing could stop the downward course of the mark.

Table 10, showing the dollar quotations on the Berlin Stock Exchange at regular intervals (without regard to intermediary fluctuations) gives some idea of a phenomenon unprecedented in history. It was as fantastic in reality as the figures look. In this chaos the German people had to live for several years.

TABLE 10

Dollar Quotations

(monthly average)

July, 1914	4.2 marks
Jan., 1919	8.9*
July, 1919	14.0
Jan., 1920	64.8
July, 1920	39.5
Jan., 1921	64.9
July, 1921	76.7
Jan., 1922	191.8
July, 1922	493.2
Jan., 1923	17,972.0
July, 1923	353,412.0
Aug., 1923	4,620,455.0
Sept., 1923	98,860,000.0
Oct., 1923	25,260,208,000.0
Nov. 15, 1923	4,200,000,000,000.0

* Computation in terms of Swiss quotations.

The table shows clearly that the turn to progressive deterioration occurred in July, 1921, with the London Ultimatum. The legendary inventor of the chess game,

German Economy

wishing to demonstrate to the Shah of Persia the effects of a geometrical progression, is said to have asked of him as a favor to have his chessboard heaped with corn in such a way that one grain was put on the first field, two on the second, four on the third, and so on in geometrical progression up to the sixty-fourth field. The Shah soon realized that there were not enough grains of corn in the world to fill the sixty-fourth field alone. This legend became a bitter reality in the German inflation.

SOARING PRICES AND LAGGARD CIRCULATION

In the first period of inflation there actually was a considerable time lag between the movements of internal and external money value; that is, commodity prices rose much more slowly than foreign exchange. In the period of irresistible devaluation prices adapted themselves ever faster and more closely to the lead of the Devisen quotations. Finally, after 1922, when the entire nation had begun to realize the connection between Devisen quotations and price movements, adjustment was more and more automatic.

Accordingly, the dollar became the ultimate measure of values in Germany; it was the decisive factor in setting German prices. The daily dollar quotations took the place of the weather as a topic for small talk. Every guttersnipe was accurately informed as to the daily dollar quotation—and of course every merchant had it at

152

The Weimar Republic

his fingertips, until at last he automatically adjusted his prices to the dollar, anticipating as far as possible the imminent further rise. It became customary to close the shops at lunchtime in order to be able to open in the afternoon with new prices, after the dollar quotation of the day had become known.

A comparison of the Devisen index with the index of wholesale prices clearly demonstrates the growing speed of adjustment (Table 11). The lag of retail prices also was diminishing.

TABLE 11

Index of Depreciation
measured by the

	Devisen	Wholesale prices
Jan., 1913	1.0	1.0
Jan., 1920	15.4	12.6
July, 1920	9.4	13.7
Jan., 1921	15.4	14.4
July, 1921	18.3	14.3
Jan., 1922	45.7	36.7
July, 1922	117.0	101.0
Jan., 1923	4,279.0	2,785.0
July, 1923	84,150.0	74,787.0
Aug., 1923	1,100,100.0	944,041.0
Sept., 1923	23,540,000.0	23,949,000.0
Oct., 1923	6,014,300,000.0	7,095,800,000.0
Nov. 15, 1923	1,000,000,000,000,0	750,000,000,000.0

So rapid was the pace of depreciation that the volume of money in circulation began to lag behind the external depreciation of the mark in terms of dollars, particularly

German Economy

after the middle of 1921. Table 12 shows the banknote circulation computed in gold marks.

TABLE 12

Banknote Circulation
(gold marks)

Average 1913	6,070,000,000
Jan., 1920	3,311,000,000
July, 1920	7,428,000,000
Jan., 1921	5,096,000,000
July, 1921	4,745,000,000
Jan., 1922	2,723,000,000
July, 1922	1,730,000,000
Jan., 1923	173,000,000
July, 1923	168,000,000
Aug., 1923	282,000,000
Sept., 1923	752,000,000
Oct., 1923	300,000,000

The paradoxical situation indicated by these figures can best be explained as follows: The increase in note circulation progressed at such a rate that, notably in the last phases of the inflation, the printing presses literally failed to keep up the required tempo. In the last months before the collapse more than 300 paper mills worked at top speed to deliver notepaper to the Reichsbank, and 150 printing companies had 2,000 note presses running day and night to print the Reichsbank notes. Even with this mass production it was impossible to prevent disturbances in the money supply of the public. As prices followed the Devisen in ever closer relation, the turn-

The Weimar Republic

over of commodities had to be handled with an ever shrinking money supply, a process to be explained only by the ever accelerating velocity of circulation. As cash in hand was exposed to daily, later even hourly, depreciation, everybody took the utmost care to hold as little of it as possible. Money in the purse burned like fire, and everyone thought only how to get rid of it at the earliest opportunity—if possible, the very minute in which it was received. While the impoverishment of the public went on, there was actually a general scramble for goods.

As shown above, the inflation was caused not only by the credits the Reichsbank granted to the Government, but also by its inflationary credits to business. In itself this would hardly have been exceptional. Inflationary credits from a central bank or from commercial banks to business constitute a "normal" source of inflation. But what made them a special economic and social feature in the German inflation period was the fact that owing to the rate of money depreciation credits granted in paper marks became a secure and abundant source of profits, and finally led to the forming of new gigantic fortunes.

The technique was simple. Industrialists took advantage of short-term bank credits not only to keep their shops going, but also for investments in other "physical values," which means that they immobilized these credits by extending their own plants or acquiring new

German Economy

plants. When the time came to repay the credits, they were so much depreciated that the buyers got for practically nothing the new plants or the material with which these plants were built and equipped. For German business this was a time of hectic activity, to the limit of available material or labor.

Of course the demand for these magic credits increased by leaps and bounds, and private interest rates rose to astronomical heights. In other words, a progressively higher devaluation factor was calculated into the interest rate. Still, as a rule, this devaluation premium lagged far behind the actual devaluation, mainly because the Reichsbank as the ultimate source of credit held the interest rates under continuous pressure by giving a large volume of business credits on short-term bills at incredibly low interest rates.

The Reichsbank started this policy of pumping inflationary credits into business, apart from the inflationary credits to the Government, in 1922. At the end of 1921 the sum in commercial bills and acceptances in the Reichsbank portfolio was only 1,100,000,000 marks. By the end of 1922 it had risen to 422,000,000,000, compared with a holding of Reich Treasury bills of 1,185,000,000,000. This means that the Reichsbank increased the inflationary effects of the credits to the Reich Government by no less than one-third through credits to private business. Approximately the same ratio between Reichsbank credits to the Reich and those

156

The Weimar Republic

to private business was kept up in 1923, the year of the highest inflation fever and of the Ruhr struggle.

But the most objectionable feature of these inflationary business credits was the interest rate at which they were granted. Up to July, 1922, the Reichsbank stuck to a discount rate of 5 per cent, then it began to advance it slowly. In August, 1923, the discount rate was still only 30 per cent; in September, 1923, it was raised to 90 per cent, at which point it was held until the end of inflation. This means that the Reichsbank calculated a devaluation premium of from 25 per cent to 85 per cent per annum, while the actual devaluation rate was more than 3,000 per cent in 1922 and several million and billion per cent in 1923.

INFLATION PROFITEERS

Accordingly, whoever possessed the ability and the necessary banking connections to procure a maximum of commercial credits and to invest them rapidly in "physical values" could amass a huge fortune in no time. The most typical example for this process and generally for the trend of capital accumulation in this period was the "Stinnes case."

Hugo Stinnes was by no means one of the "newly rich," as were so many other inflation figures. He was heir to a large and reputable coal-mining and shipping firm, and he had become a dominating figure in the

German Economy

Rhenish-Westphalian heavy industries already during the World War. When the war started, he was in control of the Deutsch-Luxemburgische Bergwerksgesellschaft, one of the largest German steel and coal-mining companies, and of the Rhenish-Westphalian Electricity Company, the leading power company of Germany's foremost industrial area. But not until the postwar inflation did the Stinnes group become the world-famous octopus.

The means by which this group was built up were procured in part from the indemnities paid by the Reich for the properties ceded in Alsace-Lorraine, in part from inflation credits. On the one hand, Stinnes made use of these means in 1920 to expand his group inside the heavy industries by forming a "community of interests" (*Interessengemeinschaft*) with another large group, the Gelsenkirchener Bergwerksgesellschaft; and again in the same year by forming a "community of interests" with the powerful electricity group of Siemens-Schuckert. On the other hand, he began to buy up promiscuously a great number of various "extraneous" companies, including banks, hotels, paper mills, newspapers, and other publishing concerns.

Parallel with Stinnes's economic influence grew his political importance. Stinnes was among the very few German businessmen—Walter Rathenau, more or less, occupying a similar position at the opposite political pole—who were courageous enough to step down into

The Weimar Republic

the political arena in person and exercise in the open the political influence inherent in their economic position. He did this both as one of the leaders of Stresemann's Deutsche Volkspartei (German People's party) and through a daily paper he had recently acquired, the *Deutsche Allgemeine Zeitung*.

Stinnes died almost immediately after the stabilization of the mark in April, 1924, just in time to save his reputation. For with the end of the inflation period these inorganic giant agglomerations of industry were doomed. As soon as inflation was followed by stabilization, prices inevitably began to decline, and as the nominal value of the huge debts incurred remained unchanged, the burden became overwhelming. With uncanny speed the whole structure built up by Stinnes crashed after his death. The Stinnes family retained a relatively insignificant residue of the former group of industries, and the whole concern disintegrated into its elements, except the "community of interests" between the Deutsch-Luxemburgische Bergwerksgesellschaft and the Gelsenkirchener Bergwerksgesellschaft, which was maintained under different management and later formed the nucleus of the German Steel Trust.

INFLATION VICTIMS

While thus on the one hand immense fortunes were accumulated, on the other, broad strata of the middle

German Economy

classes were pauperized. All property invested at fixed money values—for instance, government bonds, mortgages, mortgage bonds, and savings-bank deposits—became valueless, and thereby a class was condemned to economic annihilation that in prewar Germany had played an important role socially and politically.

After the end of the inflation attempts were made to repair, at least in part, the havoc wrought in the political and social life of Germany by the pauperization of the rentier class. By law all long-term money debts were "revalued" at a certain percentage of their original gold value. Mortgages were revalued at 25 per cent, all other debts at smaller percentages. But this law was insufficient to repair the estrangement between the young Republic, held responsible for this catastrophe, and the rentier class, the more so since the ones to advocate most energetically some revaluation legislation were the anti-Republican parties of the Right, whereas the Republican parties of the Left showed little understanding of the social and political problems involved.

With the progress of inflation the number of victims grew faster and faster, and the number of profiteers diminished. In the first phases industry and trade had benefited much more by the boons immediately resulting from each wave of rising prices than they had been harmed by the accompanying unfavorable effects. Since at that time the prevailing domestic price level lagged far behind prices abroad, the margin worked as a wel-

The Weimar Republic

come incentive to trade with other countries. This at first gave the inflation period the appearance of an industrial boom, at least as far as volume of production and employment were concerned. This boom was not even interrupted by the world depression of 1921.

Only very slowly, in many instances not until the inflation had ended, did German industry and trade realize that the flowering of business in the "inflation boom" had been only imaginary. The great "bargain" turned out to be little more than a big liquidation sale. There was never any difficulty in getting rid of goods; as has been shown, they were literally pulled out of the hands of the tradesmen. But since reproduction costs always exceeded selling prices, stocks kept dwindling, and plants were worn down. In addition, owing to the dominant position of the producer over the consumer both at home and abroad, the incentive to technical progress disappeared.

Gradually it was realized by everybody that the industrial boom was fed chiefly by a waste of substance. Soon workers and employees began to notice that they secured good general employment only by accepting decreasing real wages. Although the unions invented more and more ingenious devices to adapt wages to rising prices immediately, in this breath-taking race the advantage of prices over wages became greater and greater.

Finally the collapse of the monetary system became

161

German Economy

complete, and the disaster of depreciation overtook all and sundry. Money was no longer able to fulfill its proper function in a modern economic system. Consequently, some people reverted to primitive economic methods, such as the bartering of goods. Foreign money flowed into domestic circulation. Calculations in business and every kind of economic relation became more and more confused. Finally, the disturbances in all parts of the economic mechanism had become so serious that, despite a further rise in prices, industrial unemployment began to grow.

3. STABILIZATION

By the autumn of 1923 fundamental reform of the currency system had become a matter of life or death. How was the transition from an inflated to a stable currency to be brought about? Huge obstacles lay in the path, of which the following were the most thorny:

1. At no other time and in no other country had the currency and the faith in its functioning been so completely undermined as now and here. But without "initial confidence" no new currency could possibly be built up. Without this confidence, the circulation of the new currency also would rapidly accelerate, which would spell a new depreciation.

2. There seemed no hope of a foreign loan, which in other cases had been the chief instrument in bringing

The Weimar Republic

about a stabilization after the domestic gold reserves of a country had been depleted.

3. The central problem was how to procure resources for the initiation of the new currency. The printing press had become by far the most important source of income for the Reich Government. How could normal sources of government income be opened? How could the Reich Government be given sufficient working capital to tide it over the interim until the taxes once more began to flow regularly? During this interim it was just as impossible to place a domestic as a foreign loan.

4. Every possible currency reform presupposed at least an armistice in the fight over reparations, and a breathing-spell in reparation payments. As long as the Ruhr struggle continued, stabilization was unthinkable.

After the Ruhr struggle had been abandoned in September, 1923, and after negotiations between the occupying powers and the Ruhr industries had been initiated —which was equivalent to an armistice in the conflict over reparations—all other problems seemed solvable with the aid of some imagination, even the particularly thorny task of stabilizing the currency while still resorting to the printing press for the immediate financial needs of the Government. To overcome these difficulties, a simple trick was applied.

As mentioned above, in the last phases of the inflation the cash resources of the population had dwindled to

German Economy

an infinitesimal amount when expressed in gold. It could be taken for granted that these cash reserves would re-assume normal dimensions from the very moment the public became convinced that further depreciation was no longer imminent. An increase in the circulation up to the new saturation point of cash reserves held by the public would thus have no inflationary effects, but would merely prevent a deflationary pressure on prices. A fairly wide margin existed for the Government to provide intermediary resources by means of the printing press without incurring the danger of new inflationary symptoms.

THE "MIRACLE OF THE RENTENMARK"

This offered the theoretical solution of the problem. To make it practical, nothing was required but to convince the public that the new currency was secure against new inflationary dangers. This was achieved by the psychological trick that has been written into history under the label "the miracle of the Rentenmark."

The logical construction of the Rentenmark has some resemblance to the assignats of the great French Revolution. In the case of the assignats the "backing" of the money consisted of real estate. In the case of the Rentenmark it consisted of the "real-estate debts" of the agrarian population and of analogous debt titles of in-

164

The Weimar Republic

dustrial enterprises. In both cases the backing was purely fictitious, since it could neither be used abroad as a reserve to regulate foreign exchange nor liquidated at home. But more important than the similarities between the assignats and the Rentenmark was a dissimilarity in a decisive respect: whereas the fictitious backing was used in the case of the assignats to cover up inflationary designs, it was used in the case of the Rentenmark to give a psychological prop to the stabilization of the currency.

The idea of the Rentenmark had many originators, as frequently happens with ideas that are "in the air." There was a "Minoux Plan" that contained the first germs of the mature idea. The former Secretary of the Treasury, Karl Helfferich, propounded an idea that had much resemblance to the ultimate plan; he wanted to create a "rye mark," a currency whose unit was to be expressed in rye instead of gold, although this is a commodity that fluctuates widely in value from year to year according to the outcome of the crops. Hilferding, the Finance Minister of the first Stresemann Cabinet, replaced rye by gold. Finally Hans Luther—at that time Food Minister, a few days later Finance Minister, later Reich Chancellor (in the days of Locarno), then Schacht's successor as president of the Reichsbank, having to relinquish this position at the accession of the National Socialist regime for the ambassadorship in

German Economy

Washington—proposed a "soil mark," which, except in name, was the same thing as the Rentenmark.[3]

This stage was reached on September 17, 1923. Nine days later resistance in the Ruhr Basin was abandoned; on October 15 the Rentenbank Decree was published; and on November 15 the new currency system was finally put in force. In these two months, when the new currency system had actually already been proclaimed, the gold value of the mark had further deteriorated from several hundred millionths of a gold mark to one million-millionth. That in the end, on November 15, the German currency could be stabilized at the rate of 1,000,000,000,000 paper marks for 1 gold mark or Rentenmark gave Germany at least a title to uniqueness.

The German currency was reconstructed in the following way: The Reichsbank retained its functions fully as a bank of issue, but it was prohibited from further rediscounting Reich Treasury bills (only genuine commercial bills remained eligible, as in prewar times). Furthermore, a second bank of issue was created under

---

[3] This whole quarrel about the "coverage" of the new currency was utterly unrealistic and based either on gross misconception of the nature and function of a modern currency or on psychological motives with the purpose of creating "confidence." During the whole inflation period the Reichsbank had retained a certain amount of gold (eventually it had dwindled down to a few hundred million marks), which was not the slightest check against the disintegration of the mark amidst the floods of paper that were poured out by the printing press. If the Reichsbank had dared to touch this gold, it would only have disappeared as fast as a drop in a bucket. What actually stabilized the new mark was not the restoration by the Dawes Loan of a substantial gold holding of the Reichsbank, but the balancing of the budget.

The Weimar Republic

the name of the Deutsche Rentenbank. It was nominally provided with a "capital" of 3,200,000,000 Rentenmarks, not one pfennig of which, however, was actually paid in, as it consisted exclusively of agricultural "soil debts" and analogous obligations of industrial enterprises. These obligations bore interest to the Rentenbank, through whose receipts (representing actually a special taxation of agriculture and industry) the Rentenbank was gradually to acquire a capital of its own. The Rentenbank's claims on agriculture and industry served as "collateral" for a maximum of 2,400,000,000 Rentenmarks, which the Rentenbank could issue in the form of "Rentenbank notes" (*Rentenbankscheine*). They were legal tender circulating side by side with the Reichsbank notes. Half of the maximum amount of Rentenbank notes—1,200,000,000—was to be issued in credits to the Reich Government, the other half in credits to business through the Reichsbank.

But the first question was not whether the covering was fictitious or genuine, but whether the public could be convinced of the "stability of value" (*Wertbeständigkeit*)—the expression in fashion at the time—of the new currency. And this was actually accomplished, chiefly because it proved possible to execute the whole plan from beginning to end according to schedule. The Rentenmarks flowed into the gap created by the shrinkage of the cash holdings of the population. The Reich Government received its credit of 1,200,000,000 Ren-

German Economy

tenmarks to help finance the period of transition before the taxes would again begin to flow.

This favorable state of affairs was disturbed for a very short time in December, 1923, when the Reich Government made a "proposal" to the board of directors of the Rentenbank to increase to 1,600,000,000 Rentenmarks the credit granted to the Reich. At once the foreign exchanges began to rise again. But the board of directors turned this proposal down. This was undoubtedly the right thing to do under existing circumstances, and contributed strongly to the establishment of new confidence in the stability of the currency. In due time it appeared that the taxes, after having at last been put on a stable currency basis and slightly raised at the end of 1923, were beginning to yield returns sufficient to re-establish a balanced budget. This was of course facilitated by the temporary breathing-spell in reparation payments.

4. PLANS FOR REPARATION PAYMENTS

THE DAWES PLAN

In October, 1923, the President of the United States, Calvin Coolidge, took up a suggestion previously made by Secretary of State Hughes that the reparation problem be submitted to an inquiry by nonpolitical experts. On November 30, 1923, after the Ruhr struggle had

The Weimar Republic

been abandoned and a sort of armistice concluded in the Ruhr Basin, the Reparation Commission nominated two committees of experts to study the reparation problem and to propose (although this was not officially required) a new order of reparation payments. The more important of these committees worked under the chairmanship of General Charles C. Dawes, later Vice-President of the United States. On April 9, 1924, after careful studies the Dawes Committee laid a new reparation plan before the Reparation Commission. A few days later it became evident that peace in the reparation struggle had thereby been assured for some time to come. The plan was forthwith accepted by the Reparation Commission, and immediately afterward by the German Government. In May, 1924, after general elections in France, the Poincaré government, which had waged the Ruhr conflict, was replaced by Herriot's Cabinet of the Left. In July a conference on reparations assembled in London, in August the plan was accepted by all the governments concerned, and on September 1, 1924, it went into force.

Although the Dawes Plan was to be considered merely as a provisional solution of the reparations problem—this was emphasized in the plan itself in that no definite sum was settled for total reparation payments—it had two decisive merits as compared with all former reparation settlements. First, it replaced the fantastic annuities of former plans by amounts that seemed bear-

German Economy

able, at least for the first few years, and by this token seemed to guarantee a fair period of quiet relations between Germany and the Allies. Second, it was acknowledged by the plan that Germany needed a pause for recovery. The experts realized that the German economy, after almost a decade of the most harrowing experiences, must be granted a respite in which to produce the surplus goods required for delivery abroad. This respite was to be divided into two periods, one of quasi-total indulgence and one of a partial resumption of payments.

In the first period, planned for one year, September 1, 1924, to August 31, 1925, Germany was expected to mobilize only 200,000,000 marks from her own resources. Besides, to procure the necessary means to keep up the reconstruction of devastated war areas in France and Belgium and the interest payments to the United States, an international loan of 800,000,000 marks (about $200,000,000) was to be floated with Germany as debtor—the so-called Dawes Loan. The service of this loan, however, was to be deducted from, not added to, the regular annual reparation payments. The direct German payments and the proceeds from the Dawes Loan were supposed to net 1,000,000,000 marks in the first reparation year. In the second term the German payments were to increase from year to year; from 1,220,000,000 marks in 1925-26 to 1,500,000,000 in 1926-27, 1,750,000,000 in 1927-28, the "normal an-

The Weimar Republic

nuity" of 2,500,000,000 being reached in 1928-29, the fifth year. But even this "normal annuity" should not be regarded as a maximum. On the contrary, the plan provided that the Allies were to participate in an increase in German business as measured by a complicated "prosperity index." (A depression index was not provided for.) The bases of all the business indices from which the "prosperity index" was derived were, of course, extremely low immediately after the inflation.

A whole system of safeguards was built into the plan. The sources from which reparation payments should be derived and the sum to be taken from each source were narrowly determined. Part of the payments was to come from budget sources, for which specific custom receipts and taxes were "mortgaged." As a special source of reparation income a transportation tax was provided for. Another source of income was 5,000,000,000 marks in bonds secured by a first mortgage on all large German industrial enterprises. Another 11,000,000,000 marks in bonds were issued on the collateral of a first mortgage on the property of the Reich railways. Interest at 5 per cent and amortization of 1 per cent were to be serviced by the mortgagors. To secure the obligations of the Reich railways, the Reich Railway Company was reorganized as an autonomous corporation and "internationalized." This meant that the management was to be independent of the Reich Government, and to include foreign experts. By a similar device the

German Economy

Reichsbank was to be safeguarded against a repetition of inflation experiences. Finally, the post of a General Agent for Reparations, with headquarters in Berlin, was created. His task was to supervise the execution of the reparation obligations and to report at regular intervals to the Reparation Commission on the economic and financial situation of Germany and on the specific situation of the mortgaged assets. To this post the American expert Mr. Parker Gilbert was appointed.

For five years the Dawes Plan worked with admirable precision. All payments were made promptly and exactly on the appointed days in the agreed amounts. All "safeguards" functioned, all sources of revenue delivered the expected payments. That in the beginning of 1930 the Dawes Plan was supplanted by the Young Plan was by no means a consequence of Germany's inability to fulfill the Dawes obligations. It merely expressed the general wish to replace the "provisional" Dawes Plan by a "final" reparation plan.

When at last Germany and the Allies agreed on the desirability of making a final plan for reparation payments, the general political situation of the world had changed completely from what it had been in 1924. The Allies were no longer animated by a spirit of victory and revenge, and Germany, although disarmed, had regained her position as a Great Power. She had a right, therefore, to expect some further whittling down of her reparation obligations. But from the beginning of

The Weimar Republic

the controversy an insurmountable obstacle had barred the way to a plan substantially milder in the amount and timing of payments. This obstacle was that the Allies insisted upon maintaining a close connection between reparation payments and inter-Allied debts, although the United States absolutely refused to recognize this connection. Since the Allies were not ready to depart from the principle of having their debts to the United States paid by Germany, in fact if not in form, they made any substantial reduction in their demands contingent upon equivalent concessions by America. Thus an attempt was made to shift the responsibility for a reasonable solution of the whole problem to the United States. This attempt, of course, was bound to fail.

THE YOUNG PLAN

In essence, the Young Plan was meant to carry out this policy. After prolonged negotiations in Paris, the Young Plan was agreed upon between Germany and the Allies on January 30, 1930, the date on which the first "normal year" of the Dawes Plan was to start. The Young Plan was based upon the recommendations of a committee of experts, headed again by an American expert, Mr. Owen D. Young, chairman of the General Electric Company. It was supposed to set up a final schedule of payments, which it did by making the annuities terminate in 1988 (!). For the first two years the

German Economy

plan provided for a considerable reduction—from 2,500,000,000 to 1,700,000,000 marks—each year. Then in slow progression the maximum annuities were to be reached in 1965-66 at 2,429,000,000 marks annually. After that a degression was to bring annuities down to 898,000,000 marks in the last reparation year, 1987-88. The discounted "present capital value" of these annuities amounted to a little less than 37,000,000,000 marks, in itself a remarkable reduction from the fantastic sum of 132,000,000,000 marks fixed by the Reparation Commission in 1921. The connection with the inter-Allied debts was maintained in that the German annuities would be reduced by two-thirds of any reduction in the American claims on the Allies up to 1965, and by the entire reduction after that year.

The Young Plan not only allowed for a substantial immediate reduction in reparation payments; it also freed Germany from the humiliation of foreign controlling agencies. The General Agent for Reparations disappeared, the foreign directors were recalled from the boards of the Reichsbahn and the Reichsbank, and Germany regained full sovereignty over these two institutions. In place of the controlling agencies the Bank for International Settlements in Basle, Switzerland, was founded to work as a reparation bank on the one hand, as a sort of "central bank of central banks" on the other. This second function was prevented from developing into something tangible by the outbreak of the inter-

The Weimar Republic

national banking crisis that immediately followed the setting up of the B.I.S.

From the German standpoint these advantages of the Young Plan were offset by a project to "commercialize" part of the reparation obligations. This was, in fact, the plan's main feature for the Allies, who hoped by this expedient to raise very substantial amounts on the capital markets of the world, particularly in the United States. Allied circles at that time favored the idea of a huge international loan, whose interest was to be serviced by Germany and credited to her on the reparation account. This would have been an arrangement similar to the Dawes Loan. But it was based on a twofold illusion. In the first place, it was expected that a large sector of reparation payments could thus be eliminated from the political sphere and turned into a purely "commercial" obligation. It was furthermore believed that commercial debts are safer than political debts—under whatever conditions and up to whatever amount. It is true indeed that the National Socialist Government continued to fulfill the obligations of the Dawes and Young loans a long time after having repudiated all reparation obligations. But this success of the Young Plan was due to the fact that "commercialization" was secured for merely a small fraction of the reparation payments. The Young Loan issued in June, 1930, netted as much as 1,200,000,000 marks. But the issuing of fur-

175

German Economy

ther portions was checked by the outbreak of the "Great Depression."

5. PROSPERITY

The Dawes Plan initiated a period of recovery unparalleled in scope and intensity. The promoters' era of the 1870's had been indeed somewhat similar in character. But at that time Germany stood at the end of a victorious war, while now prosperity followed upon a crushing defeat. At the earlier time prosperity was stimulated by the influx of a war indemnity of more than 4,000,000,000 marks, while this time Germany had to pay a war indemnity unheard of in the history of any country.

The economic recovery in the second phase of the Weimar Republic was characterized by a process usually called in Germany "rationalization." Germany at that time was decidedly orienting her economic and technological policy on American patterns. America was, so to speak, discovered for the second time. After having been practically cut off for a decade by war and inflation from competition in world markets and even from knowledge of foreign developments (only a few were able to procure foreign exchange to pay subscriptions to foreign scientific or technological magazines, even fewer for traveling abroad), Germany had to discover that the world had meanwhile not stood still, and

The Weimar Republic

that America in particular had seen the development of production methods far superior to what was known in Germany. A pilgrimage to the United States began in order to gaze admiringly at the "American economic miracle."

And indeed, Germany succeeded in learning quite a lot during the six or seven quiet years that followed the catastrophe of war and inflation. Her industries managed to attain once more an amazing standard in technological equipment, and to regain the leading position in those branches in which she had led before the war—the chemical, electrical, and optical industries, and partly engineering and the textile industries, although other industrial countries had been able to take advantage of the relative autarchy of the war and inflation period to build up competitive domestic industries in these lines.

It is not merely a figure of speech to say that in these seven fat years a new Germany was built up. This is true not only of the industrial sphere. Urban housing stimulated by state subsidies experienced an unexampled expansion. Side by side with the old and ugly "rent barracks"—the German equivalent of the English and American slums—new, bright, tasteful, sometimes artistically noteworthy settlements of hitherto unknown type sprouted up, large-scale or small-scale buildings that exhaled the air of a new era of improving social wisdom. The municipalities competed with one another

German Economy

in playgrounds, swimming-pools, schools, and hospitals. Transmission lines of electric power were vastly expanded all over the country; highways were modernized, although they still lagged far behind the American standard. The merchant fleet ceded to the Allies in accordance with the peace treaties was almost completely replaced; at the end of 1930 it had nearly regained the 1914 size (4,364,000 gross registered tons as against 5,134,700 gross registered tons). But the new merchant fleet had the advantage of consisting mainly of new and accordingly much more effective units. Finally, in these years construction was begun of the foremost ocean giants of the time, the *Bremen* and the *Europa*. In 1926 already German exports had regained the prewar level of more than 10,000,000,000 marks; in 1929 they exceeded the 1913 figures by 34 per cent, despite the loss of territory in Europe and of all colonies.

How could the "miracle of reparations" happen? How was it possible that this country, which in the first years after the war had been thrown into the abyss by the load of reparations, now was able not only to maintain reparation payments but at the same time to achieve recovery unprecedented in her economic life, a real reconstruction and modernization? Although in the prosperity period reparation obligations were honored exactly according to schedule, history has never answered unequivocally whether Germany was at all

The Weimar Republic

able to pay reparations. Neither the political nor the theoretical controversy over her ability to pay has ever been decided.

During the inflation period Germany really made reparation payments out of her own resources, without the crutches of foreign capital. But then her currency and finances were completely ruined. In the period following the inflation, reparation payments left Germany's currency unimpaired, but hardly one penny of these payments came from Germany's own resources. During this entire period a steady stream of foreign capital poured into Germany, much larger than the stream flowing out of Germany in the form of reparation payments. Germany's reparation payments under the Dawes and Young plans, from September, 1924, up to the Hoover Moratorium in July, 1931, amounted in all to 10,821,000,000 marks. Against this outflow Germany's private and public indebtedness abroad, most of which originated in this same period, amounted to something over 20,500,000,000 marks. To this might be added approximately 5,000,000,000 marks of direct foreign investments in Germany. The latter, however, were more than offset by approximately 10,000,000,000 marks of German capital investments abroad.

We thus arrive at the conclusion that in the "prosperity era" from 1924 to 1930 Germany succeeded in financing not only her reparation payments but also her financial and agricultural reconstruction and the

German Economy

expansion of her economic setup. The greater part of the foreign credits came from the United States. And paradoxically enough, this vast inflow of foreign funds was one of the immediate effects of the reparation scheme. The mere fact that a General Agent of Reparations residing in Berlin, together with the Transfer Committee (both instituted under the Dawes Plan), had to watch over German finances, and especially over the stability of the German mark, inspired the capitalist world with such extreme confidence that Germany became as much the principal goal of the capital movements of that era as the United States had been in the decades before the war.

This connection between reparation payments and the influx of foreign capital was soon recognized in Germany, and political and scientific discussion revolved around the question as to what would be the fate of a country that had to incur larger and larger debts in order to keep up current reparation payments. The opponents of a "policy of fulfillment" pointed out that this whole structure of reparations and capital influx was merely a house of cards. Not the Germans, but the foreign creditors, were paying reparations. For this, Germany was currently debited with interest at high rates, which she was not paying either. The interest was simply added to the total of foreign credits. At the moment foreign credits stopped for one reason or another, the whole house of cards must collapse; it would

The Weimar Republic

then be very doubtful whether Germany would be able to pay the interest on her debt, to say nothing of the principal of the reparation payments themselves.

These arguments were countered by partisans of the "policy of fulfillment" with the thesis that the expansion of German business achieved by foreign help would in the end enable Germany to make on balance ever larger payments abroad, on both interest and reparation accounts. But before this controversy could be tested in reality, the house of cards actually collapsed.

6. COLLAPSE

In the course of fifteen years, three catastrophes befell Germany. The first, the military catastrophe in 1918, gave birth to the Republic. From the second, the utter collapse of the currency in 1923, the young Republic seemingly recovered miraculously, but in reality the social repercussions and consequences of the inflation were a continual drain on its vitality. The third and final catastrophe, the economic crisis of the early 1930's, resulted in the downfall of the Republic.

For the causes and reasons of the German crisis and its particular political implications let us look first at the agricultural situation.

German Economy

THE AGRARIAN CRISIS

The German agricultural crisis in those years was essentially a problem of the "rye belt." Rye had long been an issue in German agriculture. The annual fluctuations in the price of rye far exceeded those of other agricultural products. In years of poor crops rye was in great demand as a bread cereal and therefore brought high prices, whereas in prosperous seasons the price was determined by the amount used as cattle fodder or, if export became necessary, by the price on the world markets, which happened to be very narrow for this commodity.

In the north and the northeast of Germany there is a broad belt where rye is the dominating crop.' This belt was always especially exposed to the effects of agricultural crises, and was so exposed most grievously in the international crisis after 1929, which, with the price collapse on all commodity markets, blocked rye exports almost completely. Consequently, a large section of German peasants faced about the same conditions as the American farmers. In both countries, in Germany only as far as the rye belt was concerned, the farmers were overburdened with debts and insolvent. Both governments tried to find some solution for the debt problem and to halt the price decline by government purchases of surplus products.

But the political implications were very different in

The Weimar Republic

the two countries. By a fateful coincidence, the rye crisis was to accumulate dangerous explosives against the German Republic, although as an economic factor it had very limited importance compared with the much wider scope of the industrial and banking crisis.

This fateful coincidence was that the rye belt was largely the area of the big estates. The rye crisis was therefore the crisis of the Junkers as a class. Weimar Germany indeed had gone far to undermine the political and social power this class had certainly wielded in Imperial Germany. But the Republic never succeeded in breaking the Junkers completely. They and the groups politically and socially connected with them had a considerable share in the patronage of higher Prussian officialdom; they had close ties with the Prussian Protestant church, and, most important, with the army, which in Weimar Germany had established itself in a very independent and awe-inspiring position. And finally, it should be remembered that after 1925 a prominent representative of this social group occupied the Reich Presidency, Paul von Hindenburg.

If such a thing as a "natural enemy" of the German Republic existed, this was surely the Prussian landed aristocracy. And it might have been in the line of "historical logic" had the revolution of 1918 sequestrated the large estates and divided them up among the agricultural laborers, as had become traditional in all European revolutions since the great French Revolution. For sev-

German Economy

eral reasons the German revolution did not proceed according to this pattern. It proved important that the German Social-Democratic party, largely responsible for the revolution in its main phase, had always been almost exclusively concerned with the urban proletariat and its problems, and therefore showed very little understanding of agricultural problems. In addition, the orthodox wing of the party, in command until the World War, was sold on the idea of large-scale management in both industry and agriculture, and therefore was not in sympathy with breaking up large estates. And finally, after four lean war years the most pressing interest of the masses was to safeguard their food supply; and breaking up the great estates would certainly at first have diminished rather than increased grain production.

But once the opportunity for a revolutionary change in the traditional state of German agriculture had been missed, the later Republican Cabinets could do no more than compromise on a program of "resettlement," according to which some parts of the large estates were to be purchased and broken up under favorable conditions among farmer-settlers. The resettlement activity of the Republican governments was rather imposing. By 1931, of 5,584,000 hectares (about 13,800,000 acres) that in 1907 had been under large-scale management, 600,000 hectares (1,500,000 acres) had been transformed into settlers' farms. But on the other hand, these figures seem to show that a fundamental reform

The Weimar Republic

of the agricultural setup was not to be achieved by such methods.

One of the consequences of the survival of large estates was that the Republican governments were compelled to give financial help on a huge scale to these "archenemies of the Republic." For this they received little thanks from any quarter. It could not be made plausible to the urban masses, the chief supporters of the Republic, that the Government had to throw millions upon millions of marks into the laps of those reactionary enemies of the Republic while at the same time there were allegedly millions of unemployed asking to be settled on the lands of bankrupt Junkers. On the other hand, the landowners were by no means satisfied with the amount of government aid, and were deeply embittered because the Government took advantage of their plight and acquired more and more of their lands for resettlement. And when finally Chancellor Heinrich Brüning had the courage to prepare an emergency decree providing faster liquidation for resettlement purposes of those agricultural units which could not be restored to a paying basis despite large government subsidies, the "flimsy upper strata" of landed aristocracy made a successful appeal to the kindred feelings of the Reich President. Thus Brüning's downfall was achieved on May 30, 1932.

German Economy

THE BANKING CRISIS

In economic effect the industrial and banking crisis was much more consequential. Two reasons may be cited for the banking crisis, one of which lay in the very structure of the German banking organization.

As was explained in the first chapter, German banking had developed the mixed type of deposit and investment banks, a type of bank particularly vulnerable to crises. Such banks are incomparably more subject to market fluctuations than purely commercial banks. If in spite of this peculiar organization the German credit system weathered the storms of prewar times, it was mainly owing to their much milder nature, as compared with the crisis of the late 1920's, but also to the strong backing of the banks by substantial reserves, and their independence as to foreign credit.

One of the many unfortunate consequences of the inflation was that the banks had lost their capital almost completely. And it proved fatal that in the following recovery and boom period the banks failed to use an adequate part of the inflowing capital to strengthen their basis. Thus instead of risking only their own means, they invested their depositors' money in venturesome industrial and trading enterprises. While in prewar times the ratio between the capital funds and the deposits of the banks was about 1 to 3 or 4, this ratio deteriorated to 1 to 15 or 20 at the outbreak of the

The Weimar Republic

crisis. Thus the loss of only from 5 per cent to 10 per cent of the total assets was enough to wipe out the capital of the banks.

The second major cause of the banking catastrophe is to be found in the specific character that credits took on in the postinflation period. Exactly one-half of the credits that flowed into Germany from abroad up to 1931—10,300,000,000 marks out of a total of 20,600,-000,000—were short-term credits, and remained unconsolidated. Of these, a large quota was concentrated with the great Berlin banks, whose deposits at that time consisted of foreign moneys up to 40 per cent or even 50 per cent.

On the eve of the international crash the condition of the German banking system was such that most of the investments of the "rationalizing era"—the building and modernization of plants, the drilling of coal mines, the building of department stores and power plants—were financed by short-term bank deposits, of which, moreover, a large percentage was due foreign creditors and was ready for repatriation at the first intimation of an approaching slump.

Insiders were well aware of these weaknesses. But some of the leading bankers were wanting in a sense of responsibility, and the Reichsbank lacked the power to enforce its view. In Germany there were no legal regulations for banks, no rules for the amount of paid-in capital, for the required ratio of cash reserves, or con-

German Economy

cerning the proper activities of commercial banks. As the "bank of banks" the Reichsbank had some authority, but there was no legal way by which it could interfere in the management of other banks. It is true that Dr. Hjalmar Schacht, president of the Reichsbank from the stabilization of the mark up to the ratification of the Young Plan (which became the cause of his resignation), fought against the growing foreign indebtedness, especially if it was on short terms, but without much success. Only for foreign credits sought abroad by municipalities did the Reich Government set up an "advisory board," which had practically a veto. This enabled Schacht to apply the brakes in some cases, at least as far as the foreign indebtedness of municipalities and their widespread industrial enterprises were concerned.

Two events brought the banking crisis to a climax. The success of the National Socialist party in the Reichstag elections of September, 1930, caused the first panic among foreign creditors. It abated, however, when the Government seemed able to withstand the National Socialist onslaught. The second blow came from the Austrian banking crisis, which in May, 1931, culminated in the crash of the Austrian Creditanstalt, one of the oldest and largest international banks in central Europe. The September elections resulted in a rush of withdrawals of foreign deposits. After the Austrian

The Weimar Republic

alarm signal a general run on the banks came so swiftly that it could no longer be mastered.

The foreign governments and the central banks were by no means blind to the dangers threatening the whole international credit system as a result of these events. They tried to check the German banking crisis by two methods: by a moratorium on reparation payments, and by extending direct credits. The first method was complicated by the tie-up between reparation payments and inter-Allied war debts. Cumbersome negotiations between the Allies, the United States, and Germany had to be carried on before the Hoover Moratorium, proclaimed on June 19, 1931, could be put in force on July 7. By this act all reparation payments except the service of the Dawes and Young loans, and all inter-Allied debt payments, were postponed from July 1, 1931, to June 30, 1932. This meant virtually the end of the era of reparation payments and inter-Allied debt payments. In accepting the Hoover Moratorium Germany incurred a conditional obligation to resume reparation payments after the moratorium had expired, but this never became effective. Accordingly, after July 1, 1931, German reparation payments were confined to the servicing of the two reparation loans.

The second move in aid of Germany got under way somewhat more quickly. On June 25, 1931, the Reichsbank, whose reserves of gold and foreign exchange had been rapidly depleted since May in order to meet for-

German Economy

eign withdrawals of deposits, received a credit of 420,-000,000 marks from the central banks of England, France and the United States, and the Bank for International Settlements, to tide over the date line for payments due on June 30. This credit was prolonged time and again, until it was finally repaid in the first months of the Hitler regime.

THE GERMAN MORATORIUM

Both moves, however, were powerless to arrest the impending catastrophe. On July 13, the Darmstädter Bank was forced to suspend payments. Among the large banks the Darmstädter Bank had become involved on the largest scale in short-term financing of risky and even unsound ventures. Its insolvency followed immediately the bankruptcy of the Norddeutsche Wollkämmerei in Bremen, in which alone the Darmstädter Bank lost far more than its entire capital and reserves. After the other large banks had declared themselves unable to salvage the Darmstädter Bank, its suspension of payments threatened to lead to a general run on the banks. In this emergency the Government proclaimed a "bank holiday," which during the following few weeks was liquidated in several stages.

First, open bankruptcy of the banks had to be prevented. Although everybody was resolved to let the stockholders bear the heaviest possible losses, it was im-

The Weimar Republic

practicable to countenance the bankruptcy of institutions that were absolutely indispensable if the collapse of the entire industrial system was to be averted. Also, the small depositors could not be delivered into the hands of the liquidators. In this situation the Government chose the course (1) of guaranteeing all deposits of the Darmstädter Bank when proclaiming the "bank holiday," and (2) of putting up government money for a reorganization of the Darmstädter Bank, as well as of all other large banks. The method was to cut their paid-up capital down to fractions of the original amounts and to provide them with new stock capital, which was supplied by the Government or the Reichsbank. Only the old Berliner Handelsgesellschaft came through the crisis without government or Reichsbank aid. All the other banks actually became state banking institutions, although they remained private banks in form.

The Government pushed the banking concentration one step further. The most important amalgamation was that of the Dresdner Bank with the Darmstädter Bank, which, having tipped off the whole crisis, was the worst hit of all. It is of utmost significance that in this way the German banking system was virtually nationalized by the Republican Government just on the eve of the National Socialist revolution. For the process implied indirectly complete control of German industry by the Government.

To counter the withdrawal of foreign credits, the

German Economy

Government at the end of July, 1931, proclaimed a moratorium on short-term foreign credits. Formally arranged as a short-term "standstill agreement" between foreign creditors and German debtors, it has since been renewed at regular intervals. This was absolutely necessary if the cancellation of another 10,000,000,000 marks of short-term foreign credits was to be avoided. Once again such cancellation would have endangered the whole German currency and credit system.

This moratorium on foreign short-term credits was combined with rigid regulation and restriction of the foreign-exchange market. Never after 1931 was Germany able to rid herself of these exchange restrictions. After some time their hateful character was no longer much felt by the German people. And when, less than two years later, the Nazis came into power, the exchange control became as much a desirable instrument of their totalitarian policy as the control over the banking system.

The currency crisis was aggravated by a serious crisis in Germany's foreign trade. The German depression was in large degree due to a crisis in foreign trade. It has been estimated that on the average the normal rate of export of German industrial products at the end of the period of prosperity was about one-third of the total industrial output. Of three German industrial workers one lived from the proceeds of exports. By curtailing world trade, the international slump threat-

The Weimar Republic

ened the most important links in German industrial organization. From 1929 to 1933 German exports shrank from 13,483,000,000 marks to 4,871,000,000, or almost two-thirds, while imports had to be squeezed down even more. The question was now whether German exports should be protected by a slow depreciation of the mark, with a subsequent guarded inflation, or by trying to defend the old exchange parities by means of a deflationary policy. The answer was the more pressing after the pound sterling had been devalued on September 19, 1931, and several other nations had immediately followed suit.

DEFLATION

Germany had become a prisoner of her own inflation experiences. The deflation policy, upon which the authorities decided, entailed heavy sacrifices and remained largely ineffective. This was widely taken to prove that devaluation would have been a better policy in the special type of emergency that then had to be dealt with. But the horrors of the inflation of the early 1920's were still too fresh in the minds of the people to allow the Government to pursue a policy that the whole population would have interpreted as the first step toward a currency crisis, style 1923. This attitude of the public would probably in itself have nullified the hoped-for advantages from devaluation. Moreover, the

German Economy

domestic credit system would have been shaken so deeply that a domestic credit moratorium also might have become necessary.

Thus deflation seemed to offer the only possible escape from the export crisis, which in turn seemed inextricably bound up with the industrial crisis. By putting strong pressure on the domestic price level one could hope to offset the price decline in important purchaser and competitor countries. By such methods, in fact, a relative success was achieved. In 1931 exports were kept as high as 9,600,000,000 marks (compared with 13,483,000,000 marks in 1929), while imports were curtailed from 13,447,000,000 to 6,727,000,000 marks. An export surplus of almost 3,000,000,000 marks was thus achieved. In theory, the deflationary policy really seemed to open a path that in due time could lead out of the crisis, once the hurricane sweeping over the world markets (and particularly over the United States) had abated somewhat. Politically, however, it proved one of the strongest contributing factors in the downfall of the Republic.

To understand the scope of the deflationary policy as inaugurated by Brüning's government, it is well to remember that in Weimar Germany already, not only later in Hitler Germany, prices and wages were largely controlled by the state or by organizations under direct or indirect state influence. Prices were largely "political prices," wages largely "political wages." Tied up as the

194

The Weimar Republic

price system was with government decisions on the one hand and with monopolistic organizations or companies on the other hand, it had lost much of the flexibility that prices display in a free capitalistic economy. In further consequence of this rigidity the pressure on prices fell much more heavily on the narrow free sector of business than on the controlled sector—another disturbing factor in the economic balance.

The objective of the deflationary policy was to force the political prices down to the very level they would have reached automatically in an elastic system. But the difference between a natural and a politically enforced price decline is that nobody can find whom to make responsible for the former, whereas the blame for the latter is directed with full weight against the Government.

Deflationary policies are necessarily unpopular. It is true that the "consumers" are benefited. But since everybody is a consumer, most individuals are more concerned with their fate as producers than as consumers. Moreover, the business organizations and pressure groups center around producer interests. The co-operative movement, strong and excellently organized in Germany, had weighty producer interests. Paradoxically enough, even the pure consumer groups, such as state employees and rentiers, derived no pleasure from the deflation. For it was part of the deflationary policy to curtail civil-service salaries. And a government decree

195

German Economy

provided for the compulsory lowering of interest rates on all kinds of loans to a flat 6 per cent (which still was an abnormally high rate), since the capital market was too severely disorganized to allow voluntary conversions.

BRÜNING'S EMERGENCY MEASURES

So unpopular was the deflationary policy, and so fierce were the political and psychological inhibitions it encountered, that democracy, weakened as it was by growing unemployment and the ascendancy of the anti-democratic parties of the extreme Left and of the extreme Right, could not sustain the impact of this hostility. The defeat of the Hermann Müller Cabinet, the last strictly parliamentarian government of the Republic, had been due to a conflict centering on a deflationary measure—the raising of the workers' contribution to unemployment insurance (tantamount to a tax on the workers' income). The Brüning Cabinet, which followed on March 30, 1930, evaded the task of finding a parliamentary majority for its numerous deflationary measures. It resorted from the beginning to the undemocratic method of "emergency decrees" (*Notverordnungen*), technically based on Article 48 of the Reich constitution, which however was originally designed for use only in extraordinary emergencies and was obviously misused to cope with a difficult parliamentary situation. Nothing then remained of democracy

The Weimar Republic

except that, after an emergency decree had been issued, the Government had to induce a parliamentary majority by means of small gifts to one or another of the many existing parties to vote against the repeal.

In this way Brüning's Cabinet was maintained in power for two years. Meanwhile officials' salaries, wages, rents for dwellings, interest on loans, and "controlled" prices were lowered by emergency decrees. Not only did this deflationary campaign drain the democratic system of all its strength, but the task of deflation seemed to draw out in an endless perspective, because money was depreciating further and further in the most important purchaser and competitor countries.

First of all, the deflationary policy did not succeed in stopping the increase in unemployment. Workers on relief increased from 2,258,000 on March 15, 1930, the first day of Brüning's chancellorship, to 6,031,000 at the end of March, 1932. It now seemed certain that the direction of economic policy would have to be radically reversed, that salvation lay not in re-enforcing the deflationary policy, but in extending credit facilities, at the same time mitigating the inflationary consequences of such a move by government regulation of prices. It is a fact that the Brüning government was preparing such a volte-face, to be initiated by the issue of a premium loan, the proceeds of which were to be used for public works. But in the midst of the preparations for this loan, Brüning and his Cabinet were dismissed. The Ger-

German Economy

man democracy remained burdened with the full responsibility for the 6,000,000 unemployed. The escape from the economic crisis it was about to find, and for which it would not have had to resort again to "emergency decrees," was abruptly cut off.

7. GOVERNMENT AND BUSINESS IN WEIMAR GERMANY

If from the earliest phases of the National Socialist regime German business had the aspect of an immense military camp, it is well to remember that it was relatively easy to reshape in this way an organization built up gradually under the preceding regimes. There was one fundamental difference, however, between the economic regime in Weimar Germany and the one to develop under National Socialism: The economic policy of the Weimar period was still imbued with and predicated on the democratic spirit and democratic institutions.

THE HERITAGE OF THE 1918 REVOLUTION

As far as the revolution of 1918 was at all aimed at a fundamental change in the economic system, the ideas of 1918 boiled down to two demands: 1. "Councils" were to be formed and closely interwoven with the tex-

The Weimar Republic

ture of government and business organizations. 2. The "key industries" were to be nationalized.

The "council scheme" was an offspring of the Russian Revolution, which immediately preceded the German Revolution. In Russia the workers', peasants', and soldiers' councils (the soviets) had become an instrument of the Bolshevik revolution and their name and in part their ideology has since been maintained in the new state. In the dictatorial system of the "Soviet state" that is, "Council state"), however, their practical function soon dwindled to nothing.

In the German Revolution the workers' and soldiers' councils, improvised in the first days of the revolution in November, 1918, did not play a role of any importance. Where they were constituted they soon voluntarily abdicated their function in favor of the democratic constitutional system. But surviving the entire period of the Republic was a remnant of the revolution: the institution of shop councils (*Betriebsräte*), which we shall treat later.

2. The German Revolution of 1918 was carried forward by the masses of the workers, who had been schooled in the Social-Democratic ideology. In 1912, the last general election before the World War, one-third of the electorate voted the Social-Democratic ticket. For decades the "ultimate goal" of this party had been the "socialization of the capitalistic means of production." What could be more natural than that the par-

199

German Economy

tisans of these ideas, now that the Social-Democratic party had come to power, should press for their realization? They hoped for an immediate and palpable improvement in their living-conditions, so deeply depressed by war and inflation.

THE SOCIALIZATION OF KEY INDUSTRIES

An installment payment, at least, was due on the promises made by the revolutionary government, which had declared in a proclamation that "socialization was on the march." This payment was to be made by socializing the key industries, under which term at that time were comprised mining, the iron and steel industry, and power production.

To fulfill this program seemed perfectly simple, the more so as most public utilities, such as railroads, telephone, telegraph, municipal traction, gasworks, and waterworks, had almost without exception been for some time under public ownership with satisfactory results. Furthermore, most of the key industries were amalgamated and cartelized to such a degree that they were considered "ripe for socialization."

But in spite of all this, the revolution proved too weak to enforce the socialization of key industries. Yielding to the impetuous demand of the Socialist workers' organizations, in March, 1919, the revolutionary government proclaimed a "socialization act" as an initial step.

The Weimar Republic

At the same time the Law for the Organization of Coal Mining was proclaimed, followed in April, 1919, by a Law for the Organization of Potash Mining. In both these industries, as a little later in the steel industry, "autonomous authorities" were set up as a first installment on socialization.

The supreme authority for coal-mining was vested in the Reich Coal Council (Reichskohlenrat) on which the mining companies, the coal-miners, the coal-dealers, and independent experts were represented. Furthermore, the mining companies were organized in the Reich Coal Association (Reichskohlenverband), a compulsory cartel of the whole coal-mining industry in which the Ruhr Coal Syndicate had actual leadership. The Reich Coal Council was a planning body somewhat comparable to the NRA code authorities, with the purpose of deciding the amount of production and the prices. Ultimate decisions, however, were reserved to the Reich Government. The organization of the other autonomous bodies was along similar lines.

The career of these autonomous bodies was not too glorious. It soon appeared that they were but a poor compromise between the capitalistic and socialistic conceptions of economy. In the steel industry the organization soon degenerated. In coal-mining and potash-mining it was kept going during the entire Weimar period, but the merits of its economic policy always remained extremely doubtful. The way it worked out

German Economy

was that the representatives of employers and employees, who conjointly had a majority on the boards, were often ready to find solutions concerning prices and wages at the expense of the consumers. In many cases the Reich Government interposed its veto and thus forced price settlements better suited to public interests. But that rendered the autonomy of the boards purely fictitious, and eventually there was nothing left but a compulsory cartel under government supervision with respect to price-fixing.

This was about all that was done in the way of socialization. The vague promise of the Weimar Constitution of August, 1919, based as it was on a compromise between the Social-Democratic party and the so-called bourgeois democratic parties, was never fulfilled. But the economic system of the Weimar Republic, as it actually materialized in the peculiar mixture of private and state management of industry, and in the legal conditions of labor relations, certainly showed much stronger Socialist elements than the prewar economic system. The fundamental features of this system will now be described.

We have seen above that already in prewar times the Government played a much larger role in business in Germany than in the Western countries. Now there was a further considerable expansion in governmental control of business. The state railways were transferred to Reich ownership, forming the largest operating rail-

The Weimar Republic

road unit in the world. In the expansion of the power industry the states and municipalities took the lead. As far as street railways, subways, and bus lines were still privately owned they were now with only a few exceptions taken over by the municipalities, as were gasworks and waterworks, except the gasworks owned by the heavy industries.

HOUSING POLICY

Of all the governmental activities in business, housing represents the most commendable achievement. During the war residential building had stopped almost completely, and it had not been revived to any considerable extent all through the inflation period. A huge demand for houses and apartments had thus accumulated. But during the period of war economy the whole housing complex had been regulated by a series of legislative moves. All rents were officially fixed, private renting contracts were practically canceled, and tenants were accorded a permanent right of tenure for their dwellings provided they paid the set rent. In the last resort, the public authorities took over also the functions of renting agents.

Had rents been completely freed from governmental regulations at the time of the worst housing deficiency, they would have skyrocketed and created a serious social emergency. If, on the other hand, the low regulated rents had been retained for old houses and the

German Economy

building of new dwellings been left to the conditions prevailing on a free market, rents for old and new houses would have diverged widely, which also would have entailed many social difficulties. In this situation extensive public, or publicly subsidized, housing seemed the only remedy, and this remained the characteristic feature of German housing all through the Weimar period.

It may safely be stated that in this field extraordinary successes were achieved. Reich, states, and municipalities vied with one another in erecting tasteful residential buildings, which gradually changed the aspect of German cities greatly. Building was usually financed in the following way: Relatively cheap first mortgages at normal interest rates were granted up to only 50 per cent of the costs by savings banks, insurance companies, and mortgage banks (in some states, state mortgage banks were founded for this purpose), and relatively high second mortgages at almost nominal interest rates were granted by the Government, as a rule not out of borrowed funds but from the proceeds of the house-rent tax (*Hauszinssteuer*). This peculiarly constructed tax was an outcome of the inflation. Had the determination of rents been turned over to the free market, rents would soon have gone up far above prewar levels. On the other hand, house-owners netted a handsome revaluation profit as far as they were mortgage debtors, since mortgages were revalued by only 25 per cent after

The Weimar Republic

the stabilization. This revaluation profit was partly taxed away by the house-rent tax, and the Government could easily increase the proceeds of this tax by slowly raising rents above prewar standards and thereby procure more means for the housing programs. Moreover, states and municipalities carried on building activities on their own account or by taking a large share of the capital in nonprofit building societies and co-operatives.

THE GOVERNMENT AS BANKER

For subsequent developments, both political and economic, it was of great consequence that in the Weimar period the Government intensified its activities also in the banking field.

The Reich founded a bank of its own, the Reichskreditgesellschaft, which quickly rose to the rank of the "Big Four." Although a Reich-owned institution, it assumed the same functions as any private bank. Without a branch system, it nevertheless played an important role on the money market by means of its close connections with the provincial institutions. Those among the federal states which did not as yet possess state banks made up for it in the Weimar period. Furthermore, the Reich and some federal states founded several banks for special purposes, primarily for housing, such as the Deutsche Bau- und Bodenbank (German Building and Real Estate Bank), a Reich-owned institution for inter-

German Economy

mediary building credits, and several mortgage banks. The Reichsbahn too formed its own bank, the Reichsverkehrsgesellschaft (Reich Transport Company), to manage its liquid funds and to finance freight credits to large shippers. For some time a subsidiary of the Deutsche Rentenbank played a leading role in the field of long-term agricultural credits. The Rentenbank itself, after having been instrumental in stabilizing the currency, had hardly any function left, and the Reichsbank recovered its former monopolistic position as the central bank. But meanwhile the Rentenbank had begun to accumulate relatively large funds from the taxes that at first both industry and agriculture, later agriculture alone, had to pay to the bank's account. The Reich then resolved to utilize these funds to set up a bank with a special function, the Rentenbank-Kreditanstalt. This new institution was given the task of making agriculture participate in the blessings of foreign credits. The bank contracted loans abroad, mainly in America, which were passed on to the farmers by mortgage banks and state farm banks.

Finally, the Reichsbank, in order to gain more freedom of action than was permitted to it by law, founded the Golddiskontbank. In the course of the years the functions of this Reichsbank subsidiary changed many times. When founded it was a sort of auxiliary currency bank specializing in business with foreign countries, primarily in procuring Devisen credits; accordingly it

The Weimar Republic

first computed its accounts in pounds sterling. This made it in fact an institution for the financing of foreign trade. During the banking crisis of 1931 the Golddiskontbank became the instrument for the reorganization of the bankrupt banks by putting up new capital against common stock and granting credits. Later in the National Socialist era its functions consisted mainly in open-market operations in such government bills as the Reichsbank, for technical reasons, was not supposed to discount. It may be estimated that already on the eve of the 1929 slump public banks (apart from the Reichsbank and saving banks) accounted for at least 40 per cent of the total assets of all banks.

Thus long before the banking crisis of 1931 the state held a predominant position in German banking. The chief function of the German credit system, the financing of industrial and banking companies, still remained principally in the hands of private banks. But this was altered by one stroke when the banking crisis wiped out the capital of the large banks. As shown above, the Reich then took over the capital control of almost all large banks and held fast to it far into the National Socialist era. The subsequent "reprivatizing" of the large banks was of no practical consequence because meanwhile the state had assumed full control of the economic system as a whole.

German Economy

GOVERNMENT IN INDUSTRY

Government-owned industries were as a rule taken out of the framework of public administration and transformed into separate units run by private-business methods. Thus, for example, the army shops, Reich-owned long before the war, the nitrate and aluminum plants which the Reich had built during the war, the power plants and other industrial enterprises founded after the war, all were transferred to individual stock companies, and the stocks concentrated in a Reich-owned holding company, the Viag (Vereinigte Industrie Aktien-Gesellschaft), with which was combined the Reichs-Kreditgesellschaft as the financial organization. In connection with the provisions of the Dawes Plan, the Reichsbahn was transformed into a corporation with separate legal status, which issued preferred stock, took up loans, and finally, as mentioned above, founded its own special bank for the management of its banking activities.

After the war, partly as a heritage from the war economy, state control was extended to include the regulation of the prices of the most important commodities. The "autonomous" coal-mining boards, which worked under the supervision of the Reich and practically amounted to compulsory cartels under state control, were supplemented, in November, 1923, after the end of the inflation, by general cartel legislation. The object

The Weimar Republic

was not, however, to exert state control over the price and production policy of the cartels, but merely to forge an instrument that should restrain the "misuse of monopolistic power" and offset as far as possible the influence of industrial monopolies, which had been strengthened immensely by the inflation. At the center of the cartel laws stood a special court, the Cartel Court, which was similar in functions to the Federal Trade Commission of the United States, except that in Germany cartel agreements as such were not prohibited by law. This court was intended to prevent discrimination against outsiders, refractory patrons, and so on.

The most important clauses of this law provided that "every party to cartel agreements may withdraw without previous notice for valid reasons. "Valid reason" was defined as "any unfair restriction upon the economic freedom of action, particularly as regarding production, sale, or price-fixing." It was up to the court to decide what "unfair" restriction was. "Without the consent of the president of the Cartel Court no bonds may be forfeited nor may any boycott or similar means be applied in consequence of violation of the agreement." It was in the period of postinflation prosperity (1926) that the biggest and most comprehensive industrial amalgamations were perfected: the German Steel Trust and the German Dye Trust, two giants that have since maintained their predominant position. The num-

German Economy

ber of individual cartels at that time was officially estimated at twenty-five hundred.

Not until the economic crisis exerted its full pressure did the Brüning administration go one step further in providing the legal instrument for state control over the cartels and their whole policy. The cartels were included in the deflationary measures of the Brüning Cabinet, and forced to a general reduction of "fixed prices." This was, of course, not the way to restore to the price mechanism the flexibility lost through cartelization.

The problems in agriculture during the depression were the exact opposite of the industrial problems. Here the question was how to put up dams against a too rapid slump in prices. Gradually a complicated system of props was constructed in the shape of scaled import duties, import quotas and embargoes, state purchase of supplies, a state monopoly for corn, and many other sorts of regulations. These were supplemented by a special regulation for agricultural credits, mainly measures amounting more or less to moratoriums.

LABOR POLICY

In the field of labor relations, Imperial Germany bequeathed to the Republic a well-developed system of social security, built up in prewar times, and the shop-council system, which originated in the war years.

With respect to social security very little indeed re-

The Weimar Republic

mained to be done. Employees were insured against almost all sorts of contingencies. Maximum hours and minimum wages were fixed; women and children were particularly protected. All that remained was to put more teeth into some of these measures. Furthermore, in November, 1918, the first decree of the revolutionary Government of People's Commissars proclaimed the 8-hour day as the legal maximum working day.

The admirable achievements of the Bismarckian era in the field of social insurance likewise admitted of no fundamental improvements with respect to the systems of health, old-age, sickness, and accident insurance. In one field alone did the German social-insurance system prove deficient, primarily in view of the violent movements of the business cycle in the postwar era. While England had begun in 1911 to develop a system of unemployment insurance, Germany entered the war without any preparation in that respect, and only during the war was a system of doles developed, which were, however, not based on any insurance scheme but merely on actual needs. A regular unemployment-insurance scheme was not introduced in Germany until 1926. And the scheme then organized worked satisfactorily solely in times of reasonably good business. It broke down under the stress of the mass unemployment that followed the slump. Despite increasing state contributions and decreasing benefits for the insured, the number of those unemployed who received regular insurance

German Economy

payments dwindled more and more, because the contributions for the unemployment funds declined as rapidly as the outlay increased. Thus the masses of those unemployed for more than six months were once again dependent on the former dole according to needs. This was administered partly as "emergency relief" in extension of the insurance system, partly as outright dole by the local communities subsidized for this purpose by the Reich. Thus at the end of the Weimar period virtually nothing was left of unemployment insurance except a tax on the salaries to be paid by employers and employees.

MEDIATION AND ARBITRATION

The original contribution of the Weimar Republic to social reform was in the field of regulating relations between employers and employees. This was based on' two principal pillars: organized mediation and shop councils.

The practice of mediation was built upon collective bargaining between the trade-union and the employer or employers' organization for the individual industry. Whereas before the war collective labor contracts were regarded as a purely private affair of the parties concerned, under the Weimar system the collective labor contract was recognized by the state as the normal and most desirable form of regulating labor relations in the public interest.

The Weimar Republic

The term commonly used, that the trade-unions were "recognized" by the state in Weimar Germany, means that none but free and independent trade-unions had "collective bargaining and contracting power" in representing the employed; that is, both the so-called yellow unions (corresponding roughly to the company unions in the United States) and the isolated shop crews were excluded. Thus the unions had a far stronger and more secure legal position in Weimar Germany than the American unions enjoy under the National Labor Relations Act.

The official mediation authorities were charged with intervening in difficult cases of collective bargaining. They had to try to induce both parties to compromise. Whenever this mediation was successful and a collective agreement was arrived at by the good offices of the state, the character of private and free labor contracts was not impaired. But in reality mediation went far beyond these theoretical limits. In the first place, the collective agreement did not admit of "contracting out," which means that individual labor contracts with poorer conditions for the worker than under the collective agreement were not admissible. This could still be reconciled with the idea of free contract. But the Government had further rights, first, to declare a labor agreement as "generally binding," thus extending the scope of the agreement over all employers and employees of the respective industry and district, even if they had not

German Economy

participated in the negotiations for the agreement. And second—this was the most far-reaching innovation—in cases where voluntary agreements were not achieved, the mediator issued his own decision, which if accepted by only one party became just as binding for both as a voluntary collective agreement, and was legally treated as such. In this way the Government gradually assumed responsibility for all labor relations. What originally was thought of as an exception to be avoided as often as possible became more and more the rule. Decisions on wage rates were—not in every case but precisely in the most difficult, critical, and decisive cases—taken away from the parties to the bargain, and from the free interplay of their forces in the economic sphere, and were made subject to the economic policy of the Government. The fiction was kept up that the official wage decisions should amount to what the parties would have freely agreed to by reason and fairness. But it is obvious that the criteria of "reason and fairness" could not be defined otherwise than by the actual economic doctrines and intentions of the Government of the day. This applies to the extent of wage increases in the prosperity period as well as to the wage reductions in the subsequent deflationary period.

There is tragic irony in the historical development by which the German Revolution first greatly enhanced the importance, strength, and authority of the German unions, only to land them at the end of this period al-

The Weimar Republic

most in the position of administrative organs of the state, consequently deprived of their real function of constituting a powerful body of workers to face the power of the entrepreneurs.

On the other hand, by assuming responsibility for fixing "political wages," the state exposed the young German democracy to a very severe strain. In the prosperity period, the employers and a considerable part of economic journalism attacked the wage policy of the state for "overraising" the wage level. Consistently, these groups later made the state responsible for the slump that, at least in part, was due to the rigidity of the wage level. The unions at the same time occasionally hedged themselves against the workers' demands for further wage increases by shifting the responsibility to the state. Thus, as the depression deepened, the workers directed their exasperation against the state for letting wages slide, and the entrepreneurs and a large sector of public opinion attacked the Government bitterly for a wage (and price) policy that seemed to prolong and intensify the depression. And both Nazi and Communist opposition—at that time already in unholy close co-operation—did their best to arouse recklessly the passions of a despairing nation against the political regime. The German democracy thus also undermined its popular basis by shouldering tasks from which the far more strongly consolidated Western democracies have shrunk up to the present.

German Economy

INDUSTRIAL DEMOCRACY

The second and much sounder pillar on which labor relations were founded in Weimar Germany was what might be termed "shop democracy." As shown above, the one feature of the "soviet idea" that proved practicable in Germany was the institution of shop councils. The Shop Council Act of February, 1920, provided that annually in every plant with at least five employees a shop representative was to be elected, and in every plant with at least twenty employees a shop council consisting of several members. Corresponding to the method accepted at that time for political elections, the shop councils were elected by proportional representation from panels of candidates.

Since Germany in this period had three groups of trade-unions (the Free Unions, the Christian Unions, and the Hirsch-Duncker Unions), which hardly differed as to their practical methods, the system of proportional representation had the good effect of preventing interunion competition from taking on any harsh forms. In shops where the workers belonged to two or more unions, each union had its representatives in the councils.

Thus industrial relations in Germany ran along the two separate tracks of collective bargaining and the shop-council system, which made for a salutary division of labor between the unions and the shop councils. The

The Weimar Republic

unions were allotted the whole field of collective bargaining, all agreements to be reached with a group of employers—such as those on wages, hours, paid vacations, and apprenticeship. The shop councils were left in charge of all negotiations with individual employers within the framework of the collective agreements. Moreover, the councils acted as connecting links and buffers between the employees and the employers in the innumerable smaller or larger controversial matters that occur in every plant, of which the most important are the hiring and the firing of workers. As the council members themselves were protected against losing their jobs, except for compelling reasons, they enjoyed a measure of independence in their relations with the employer that constituted a prerequisite for the satisfactory working of the whole council system.

But beyond these tasks, which as a rule were fulfilled by the shop councils to general satisfaction, the councils were burdened with a heritage from the time of the "soviet idea" that brought them much less success. As a last remnant from the "soviet idea" the shop-council legislation provided that the shop council be charged "with offering its advice to the management in order to safeguard the highest possible standard and best economic performance of the shop management"; furthermore, it was provided that the shop accounts had to be put before the shop council and that the council was entitled

German Economy

to representation with voting power on the board of directors of stock companies.

It soon appeared that these clauses of the Shop Council Act were doomed to failure—on the one hand, because the employers were not interested in enforcing them, but rather made an effort to circumvent them (for example, by taking certain functions away from the boards of directors on which the shop councils were represented and assigning these tasks to special committees); on the other hand, because the shop representatives were not intellectually equipped for these tasks. But this part of the council system proved to be harmless at least.

PREPARED FOR HITLER

When it came to its end, the democratic Republic left as a heritage to the National Socialist state an economic system that corresponded rather closely to a complete system of "State Socialism." The state was, so to speak, in command of the whole blood circulation as represented in a modern economic system by the banking mechanism. The state held in its grip the most important "commanding heights" over business, such as the transportation system, the power supply, and the influence over cartel prices. The state had, furthermore, taken over vital functions of the trade-unions and the employers' organizations.

To complete the picture of how far this "penetration

The Weimar Republic

of business by the state" had gone at the end of the Weimar period, one should visualize quite clearly to what an unprecedented degree the national income was controlled and redistributed by the state in the shape of taxation, customs duties, and social-insurance contributions. It may be estimated that in 1929 from 20 per cent to 25 per cent of the national income went to the state in one way or another. In 1932, after the national income decreased more rapidly than tax and social-insurance receipts, from 30 per cent to 35 per cent of the national income was levied and distributed by the state, and if one includes the public enterprises (railroads, public utilities, building, and so on) of which prices and costs were largely determined by political and social considerations, even from 50 per cent to 60 per cent.

When at last it became apparent that this state intervention in the shape it had achieved at the height of the prosperity period was powerless to prevent the outbreak of the most disastrous economic crisis in German history, the full responsibility for the economic decline was blamed on the "system"—that is, the Weimar democracy. But paradoxically enough, it was not the system of state intervention as such that was blamed by the opposition. This system was much too deeply rooted in the German political and economic history of the last few centuries. On the contrary, the general popular feeling pressed the demand that this very imperfect and incomplete system of state intervention be superseded

219

German Economy

by one more nearly perfect and complete. This was the content of the "anticapitalistic yearning" which, according to a National Socialist slogan of the day, pervaded the German nation. In fact, after the Reichstag elections of 1930 the political parties that stood for the largest possible degree of governmental regulation of business represented the overwhelming majority of the people. The fact that every one of these parties fought for a fundamentally different kind of state regulation does not detract from the truth of the statement that public sentiment was much more in favor of increasing state influence over business than of returning to a free capitalistic economy.

This explains why the opposition against the National Socialist dictatorship was much weaker in the field of economics than in the political and cultural sphere. The road to the totalitarian state had been well laid out. The National Socialist Government needed but to utilize for its own aims the instruments of state power forged by its predecessors.

8. INTERLUDE

On May 30, 1932, the Brüning Cabinet was dismissed. This event was preceded on April 24 by elections to the Prussian Diet which resulted in a majority for the revolutionary parties of the Right and Left. National Socialists and Communists together outnumbered the

The Weimar Republic

parties in between. As they invariably voted together, a constitutional government was no longer legally possible in the dominant federal state. The Republican administration in Prussia, consisting of Socialists, Centrists, and Democrats, remained in office to continue the conduct of routine administration. It was obviously an untenable situation. As Prussia was responsible for three-fifths of the area of the Reich, chaos began to spread rapidly. This was a glaring invitation to all sorts of Putsch plans. Force had to be met with force. The legal basis of the Republican regime had become tenuous in any event.

Chancellor Brüning, who still had the support of a majority in the Reichstag, struggled hard to survive this chaotic period. His hope was pinned to a striking success in the questions of reparations and disarmament. Promising negotiations were in progress to achieve the consent of the Western Powers to a substantial increase of the German Army, within the framework of a general agreement, and the virtual repeal of reparation payments. This success should enhance the prestige of the Republican system sufficiently to enable it to make a successful offensive against the rising tide of the revolutionary forces. But before Brüning could complete negotiations he fell a victim ("a hundred paces from the goal") to a palace intrigue of the clique surrounding the venerated but senile Reichspräsident von Hindenburg.

Dr. Heinrich Brüning was replaced by Franz von

221

German Economy

Papen, who was called to establish an "authoritarian" regime, at least for a period of transition. The question of whither this transition should lead was left open. Not for a moment did Von Papen claim to be backed by a majority in the Reichstag or of the people. As a matter of fact his appointment was passionately denounced not only by the Nazis and the Communists but also by all Republican parties. His sole support came from the Deutschnationale Volkspartei of Geheimrat Hugenberg, which represented less than one-tenth of the people.

Franz von Papen was a conservative Roman Catholic, member of the Prussian Diet, owner of several conservative Catholic newspapers, a man of substantial wealth who had never played a conspicuous role in German politics and had never been taken seriously. Nevertheless, he plunged into the adventure with the utmost nonchalance, like a buoyant officer who starts a cavalry attack or enters a steeplechase. In the first weeks of his regime he reaped the fruits of Brüning's labors. He represented Germany at the Lausanne Conference, which on June 16, 1932, suspended reparation payments. (Incidentally, the Lausanne agreement was never ratified by any of the signatory powers.)

About one month later on July 20, 1932, Von Papen deposed by a coup d'état the Prussian Government, establishing himself as "Reichskommissar for Prussia," an office nowhere provided for in the constitution. The

The Weimar Republic

Prussian Government yielded without resistance, and Von Papen remained unperturbed when the Reichsgericht in Leipzig (the Supreme Court of Germany), declared the act of July 20 unconstitutional. During the same months the first signs of economic recovery, aided by both international and domestic developments, became apparent. The Lausanne Conference improved international confidence, and both Great Britain and the United States experienced some revival of business activity. At home the Von Papen government reversed the deflationist policy of its predecessors. A substantial public-works program was initiated, and private investments were encouraged by the issuance of tax certificates, a government subsidy to be amortized over a period of five years by the return from certain business taxes.

Meanwhile, the Reichstag had been dissolved on June 3, and a most passionate campaign was in swing for elections to be held on July 31. The elections resulted in an overwhelming victory for the National Socialists, who increased their seats from 107 to 230; the Social-Democrats returned with 133, the Communists with 89, out of a total of 608. It must be noted that even in these last, relatively free elections National Socialists mustered not much more than one-third of the people, but together with the Communists, in the Reichstag as before in the Prussian Diet, they had a solid majority. From a parliamentary point of view the party's position seemed ut-

German Economy

terly hopeless. But Von Papen seemed unperturbed. The following months were filled with indecisive negotiations between the clique around Hindenburg and Hitler, which led to nothing. This period increased the chaotic conditions of the country. Riots and political murders, resistance to the authority of the Government, assaults on party leaders, and uninhibited slander were rife throughout the country. Under these conditions the new Reichstag convened on August 30, only to be dissolved again on September 12. The new elections were ordered for November 6.

This time Von Papen led a valiant attack on the National Socialists, hoping to cash in on his successes. But although the Nazis suffered severe losses in the November elections—which seemed to have a demoralizing effect on the morale and the financial condition of the Nazi party—the opposition against Von Papen did not abate anywhere, and he remained as far from a parliamentary majority as before. Meanwhile, the lack of legality of the Government created a more and more revolutionary atmosphere. It became daily more threatening when a wave of political strikes began to sweep the country, being most dangerous in Hamburg and Berlin. In the instigation and organization of all these strikes Nazis and Communists again worked in hostile co-operation.

During all this time the power behind the throne was the army, represented by a political general, Kurt von

The Weimar Republic

Schleicher. When the situation seemed to become unmanageable, General von Schleicher, who had already made and overthrown Brüning and made and backed Von Papen, had finally to step to the fore himself and form a government (December 2, 1932), before the new Reichstag had assembled. He did it with no less dilettantism than Von Papen. His political aim was first to reconcile the workers embittered by Von Papen's highhandedness. Schleicher went out of his way to gain the support of the trade-unions and at the same time to split the Nazi party by winning over its left wing, headed by the popular floor-leader of the Nazis in the Reichstag, Gregor Strasser, second only to Hitler himself in popularity with the rank and file of the party. Schleicher was never given a chance to prove the workability of his political scheme. The man who had maneuvered all the political intrigues of the Republic for years was again defeated by intrigue. His former friend and protégé, Von Papen, took his vengeance. The same man who while Chancellor had fought valiantly and successfully against Hitler allied himself with Hitler after his forced retirement, and on January 30, 1933, Kurt von Schleicher was faced with the accomplished fact of a Hitler-Papen Cabinet formed behind his back by the same camarilla around Hindenburg that had shaped German destiny since 1930.

A new chapter of history had begun.

PART V

THE THIRD REICH

THE THIRD REICH

1. THE "UNALTERABLE" NAZI PARTY PROGRAM

AT ITS BEGINNING the National Socialist movement was certainly not an economic movement. However, both its initial expansion and its final coming into power occurred in periods when the privations and sufferings inflicted on the masses by economic crises were casting intense shadows over Germany, and people were looking for a system that would promise to salvage them.

The party was founded in 1920, when the Weimar regime, born of Germany's deepest humiliation, was battling in vain against the rapidly rising tide of inflation, and it took its first revolutionary action in 1923, when, during the French invasion of the Ruhr district, the German currency and with it the whole German economic system collapsed completely. For a few years the Nazi movement seemed to have faded out. In the Reichstags of the 1920's the party was represented by about a dozen members. This representation jumped suddenly to 107 at the elections of September, 1930. From then on until the end of the Republic by Hitler's appointment as Chancellor on January 30, 1933, the constitutional system of the German Republic was

229

German Economy

thrown out of function by the co-operative efforts of the Nazis and the Communists, in both the Reichstag and the most important Diets of the states, particularly in Prussia. In September, 1930, when the Nazis won the first decisive victory that made them a great power within German politics, Germany had no more than 3,000,000 unemployed. In proportion to the population this would correspond to less than 2,000,000 in Great Britain, not many more than Great Britain had even in its latest prosperity wave. Moreover, such a degree of unemployment had persisted at that time for only a few months. In October, 1929, it had still been about 1,500,-000 after years of prosperity and virtually full employment. Therefore unemployment and depression could not be primarily responsible for the rising tide of National Socialism. True, in the years immediately following the depression deepened rapidly and unemployment rose to unprecedented heights, as was shown in the preceding chapter. But even at the last elections, on March 6, 1933, held under Hitler with but scanty remnants of freedom and secrecy, the working classes and the unemployed remained loyal to the so-called proletarian parties, the Social-Democrats and the Communists, which lost hardly any votes. Thus it could not be the unemployed who brought Hitler into power.

But it was the economic crisis just the same that bred the atmosphere of despair in which a movement at once

The Third Reich

revolutionary and mystic could easily spread. It must be noted that National Socialism began to grow when the Rhineland was already completely evacuated of foreign troops, when Germany was received by the League of Nations as a member on equal status with the other Great Powers, when the Young Plan had reduced (although very inadequately) the reparations. And it came into power when reparation payments had been virtually abolished by the Lausanne Conference in June, 1932.

By denying the merits of an economic interpretation of the rise of National Socialism, we do not intend to deny that the economic argument played a large part in the propaganda of the party. The party program, the so-called Twenty-five Points, accepted in a public meeting in the Munich Hofbräuhaus on February 24, 1920, was largely an economic and social program. This program has remained the spiritual foundation of the movement. It is being taught in every school, referred to in all training courses of all the various units of the party. It constitutes, together with *Mein Kampf* by Hitler, the directing force of the intellectual concept and trend of the party. It is true that the Nazi regime, which was very consistent in the execution of the political points of the program, has not done much to fulfill its economic promises. What we consider as the essence of Nazi economics is not heralded in this program. But

German Economy

the spirit of it remains alive, and thereby a decisive element in shaping the German future.[1]

ANTICAPITALISM

The National Socialist party was from the outset an anticapitalist party. As such it was fighting and competing with Marxism. Born in a time immediately after the World War, when socialization of Germany and perhaps of all Europe seemed inevitable to many, the Nazi program attacked the problem from three angles, none of which was in any sense new or strange even to the Weimar Constitution. It was by adopting and exaggerating the principles of Weimar rather than by at-

[1] The following points of the "unalterable" party program concern economic issues: "3. We demand land and soil (colonies) for the maintenance of our people and the settlement of our surplus population . . . 7. We demand that the state shall make it its first duty to promote the industry and livelihood of citizens of the state . . . We demand therefore: 11. Abolition of incomes unearned by work. 12. In view of the enormous sacrifice of life and property demanded of a nation by every war, personal enrichment due to a war must be regarded as a crime against the nation. We demand therefore ruthless confiscation of all war gains. 13. We demand nationalization of all businesses which have been up to the present formed into companies [trusts]. 14. We demand that the profits from wholesale trade shall be shared out. 15. We demand extensive development of provision for old age. 16. We demand creation and maintenance of a healthy middle class, immediate communalization of department stores, and their lease at a cheap rate to small traders, and extreme consideration for all small purveyors to the state, district authorities, and smaller localities. 17. We demand land reform suitable to our national requirements; passing of a law for confiscation without compensation of land for common purposes; abolition of interest on land loans, and prevention of all speculation in land. 18. We demand a ruthless struggle against those whose activities are injurious to the common interest. Common criminals against the nation, usurers, profiteers, etc., must be punished with death, whatever their creed or race.

The Third Reich

tacking them that National Socialism wooed the masses. The first angle was the moral principle, the second the financial system, the third the issue of ownership. The moral principle was "the commonweal before self-interest" (Point 24). The financial promise was "breaking the bondage of interest slavery" (Point 11). The industrial program was "nationalization of all big incorporated business [trusts]" (Point 13).

By accepting the principle "the commonweal before self-interest," National Socialism simply emphasizes its antagonism to the spirit of a competitive society as represented supposedly by democratic capitalism. The masses were and are told that the capitalist doctrine requires the ascendancy of self-interest over the commonweal, while in fact the liberal philosophy of early capitalism asserts that the commonweal is best served when everyone pursues his self-interest in the most reasonable way. But to the Nazis this principle means also the complete subordination of the individual to the exigencies of the state. And in this sense National Socialism is unquestionably a Socialist system.

The principle, however, is sufficiently vague to cover all sorts of economic currents and conflicting interests. It allows the regime to pursue a policy of unbridled opportunism by simply ordering that the commonweal requires such and such measures. Thus it fosters both profit interests of entrepreneurs and utter radicalism of workers and intellectual déclassés. Discussion within the

233

German Economy

party (as far as any is permitted) is centered not around the principle but around the practical question What is the commonweal? The class struggle the party went out to suppress is only shifted into the party.

Undoubtedly, in the first year after coming into power the radical wing in the party seemed to gain strength by lining up together labor leaders, intellectuals, and the leaders of the semimilitary organizations within the party. This combination spoke of, and pushed onward toward, the second revolution. At a time when the conservative forces of the old conquered regime were still very powerful (one must not forget that Hitler came into power as the head of a coalition government) this radical trend toward a second revolution—meaning a social revolution following the political one—was extremely dangerous to the regime. The leaders of the radicals were crushed in the so-called purge of June 30, 1934. Among the hundreds of victims of this German St. Bartholomew's Day, a mass execution without trial, were several of the most prominent and conspicuous "old fighters" of the movement, among them Captain Roehm, member of the Cabinet and organizer and commander of the S.A. (Storm Troopers, Brown Shirts), and Gregor Strasser, up to 1933 the floor-leader of the Nazi party in the Reichstag. Again the primary motive of this purge was by no means economic. It was a struggle for power within the party that threatened Hitler's own position, an incipient revolt

The Third Reich

that had to be quenched before it could spread, as had happened several times before the party had seized the Government. But the effect was just the same: prevalence of the conservative over the revolutionary forces—a historical sequence most similar to the Russian events that led to the extirpation of Trotzkyism and of virtually all the "Old Bolsheviks."

BREAKING THE BONDS OF INTEREST SLAVERY

Among the many quaint slogans introduced by National Socialism this was the quaintest. Although it has disappeared almost completely from public discussion, it had probably a greater appeal to the masses in the early years of the ascendancy of the party than any other slogan. It must be realized that no historical experience, not even the defeat in the World War and the Treaty of Versailles, left such a deep impression on the minds of the German people as the utter collapse of the German currency. The years of uncontrollable inflation that followed the war seemed to have driven the German people into a hopeless fight against a monster that nobody appeared to understand, a specter that mockingly evaded every attack. The whole nation seemed to bog down into a mire from which there was no emerging. No wonder that in such a period all notions about money, banking, interest, and credit were drowned in utter confusion. Not even the responsible authorities

German Economy

remained unaffected (as is exemplified by the seriously meant experiment with a rye currency mentioned in a preceding chapter).

Only against this background of the experience of the great inflation can the economic and social ideology of National Socialism be understood. This ideology starts from the curious distinction between "creative" and "rapacious" capital (*schaffendes und raffendes Kapital*). Creative capital is essentially industrial capital, rapacious capital is finance and trade capital. The rapacious capital, so the National Socialist saga goes, has conquered all the power in modern society and subjected the people to interest slavery. By an easy political application of this theory, all Republican parties, however radical they pretended to be, were alleged to be tied up with international finance capital, whereas the National Socialist movement had realized that the redemption of the people could be achieved only by breaking the bondage of this interest slavery. And by another logical short cut, finance capital was characterized as Jewish, the creative capital as "Aryan." [2]

[2] This application of the National Socialist race theory is as irreconcilable with historical facts as the racial theory itself is with modern science. Industrial capital in Germany was represented by such noteworthy Jewish personalities as Emil Rathenau, the founder of the A.E.G. (German General Electric Company), and Albert Ballin, the founder of the Hamburg American Line. On the other hand, the Jews were a minority among the prominent "Aryans" in the domain of finance capitalism. All the great banks of Germany were founded by non-Jews—for example, the Darmstädter Bank by Gustav Mevissen, the Disconto-Gesellschaft by Julius and Adolf Hansemann, the Deutsche Bank by Adalbert Delbrück and Georg von Siemens.

The Third Reich

But the groups to whom National Socialism primarily appealed did not bother much about historical and scientific truth. They only stared at the witches' caldron of inflation, saw people growing immensely rich overnight by the simple device of borrowing money and buying commodities. They saw that only a relatively tiny number of people had access to the fountains of credit, and that an even tinier number had the power to distribute the blessings of borrowing and lending, while at the same time virtually the entire middle class, with the savings accumulated during generations, was helplessly caught in the maelstrom of a disintegrating money system and ruined. At the same time, as was shown in the preceding chapter, inflation accelerated a process of concentration of capital and economic power that fitted in any event into the trend of the present phase of capitalistic development. The little fellow felt himself more and more subdued, the craftsman by the factory, the shopkeeper by the department store, the peasant by the cattle-dealer and the grain-dealer. When at last the inflation was overcome and a new stable currency system was established, the real impoverishment of Germany became apparent, and the shortage of capital necessarily expressed itself in high interest rates. This again seemed to bear out the Nazi theories in the minds of those whom the inflation actually had expropriated and who saw themselves cut off now from the sources of credit, or oppressed by staggering debts. But long be-

German Economy

fore the National Socialists came into power the entire issue had lost its practical significance. The Republican governments, particularly the Brüning Cabinet, had already, by governmental decree, reduced interest rates, and the power of the banks was destroyed by the crisis of 1931. By the end of the Weimar period virtually the whole banking and credit system was owned or controlled by the Government.

The most curious contradiction, however, is evident in the fact that the same National Socialist movement that was to benefit so immensely from the catastrophe of the inflation was itself predicated on a strictly inflationist program. The so-called Feder money, it is true, was not included in the Twenty-five Points, but it played a paramount role in the history of the movement and remained an essential part of the Nazi policy in combating unemployment after 1933. Its name was derived from Gottfried Feder, originally the prominent and trusted economic adviser of Adolf Hitler. Feder, who dropped out of the picture soon after the Nazis had seized the reins of government, was father to the proposal that residential buildings and other public works be financed by issuing "construction money" (*Baugeld*), which was to be "secured" by the "value" of the construction so financed. It was just one of innumerable fancy monetary proposals that pop up everywhere in disturbed times and that are nowhere taken seriously by people who know anything about money and credit.

The Third Reich

When Hitler was appointed Chancellor, he made Hjalmar Schacht his responsible adviser in monetary matters, not Gottfried Feder. But what Schacht did was not much more than to adjust Feder's ideas to the more orthodox forms of the existing monetary system, and to devise an inflationist system of "work creation" within the framework of a currency technically and legally still based on a gold standard. Feder denied the inflationist character of his proposal with the argument that to the amount in which his money was issued new "values" would be created. But he overlooked the fact that this money would remain in circulation after the buildings were completed and would therefore be accumulating in volume indefinitely.

THE NATIONALIZATION OF BIG INDUSTRY

The nationalization of big industry was never attempted after the Nazis came into power. But this was by no means a "betrayal" of their program, as has been alleged by some of their opponents. The socialization of the entire German productive machinery, both agricultural and industrial, was achieved by methods other than expropriation, to a much larger extent and on an immeasurably more comprehensive scale than the authors of the party program of 1920 probably ever imagined. In fact, not only the big trusts were gradually but rapidly subjected to governmental control in Germany,

German Economy

but so was every sort of economic activity, leaving not much more than the title of private ownership. Gradually but rapidly, out of the necessity first of creating employment and afterward of building up a huge armament system, grew an economic system that made the state as much an economic dictator as it was from the beginning a political dictator.

2. NAZI ECONOMIC POLICY

In the five years between 1933 and 1938 the German economic system underwent a revolutionary change. Hitler and the National Socialist party came into power at the lowest point of the world depression, which in Germany was reached at about the same time as in the United States, at the turn of 1932 and 1933. At that time Germany had 6,000,000 registered unemployed. In the subsequent years unemployment was reduced and employment increased, as is shown in Table 13.

TABLE 13

Employment in Germany

October	Employed	Unemployed
1933	14,458,000	3,745,000
1934	16,072,000	2,268,000
1935	16,954,000	1,829,000
1936	18,279,000	1,076,000
1937	19,662,000	502,000
1938	20,838,000	164,000

The Third Reich

By spring, 1938, unemployment was virtually abolished; the state of full employment of the nation was attained. New reserves of labor have since been acquired by the annexation of Austria (March, 1938), of the Sudetenland (September, 1938), and finally by the establishment of a protectorate over the Czech and Slovak remnants of the former Czechoslovak Republic. Even in this newly acquired territory unemployment disappeared within a few months after the German troops had marched in.

How was this "miracle" achieved? By no other means than by huge public works accompanied by complete control of production, distribution, and consumption, and the virtual abolishment of freedom of movement for both agricultural and industrial workers. The purposes of this economic policy were changed in their emphasis several times. As early as the spring of 1933 Hitler, together with Hugenberg, first the leader of the conservative nationalists and then Hitler's ally, issued a proclamation promising a Four Year Plan "for the rescue of the German peasant, to maintain the nation's food supply, and to rescue the German worker by a powerful attack on unemployment." In March, 1935, general conscription was openly proclaimed, and armament, which had hitherto been organized more or less secretly, was pushed on a monumental scale. One year later, in March, 1936, Hitler sent his army into the Rhineland, which under the Treaty of Versailles and

241

German Economy

the Treaty of Locarno (1925) was pledged to remain a demilitarized zone. Immediately the fortification of the German frontier against France was started, notwithstanding the protests made to the German Government by France and England.

In 1937, four years of Nazi regime having expired, Hitler proclaimed another Four Year Plan destined to make Germany self-sufficient in food supply and industrial raw materials. A huge industry for the production of substitute materials for commodities that up to now had had to be bought abroad was to be built up. This is only another aspect of armament. This entire Four Year Plan was not meant to make things cheaper, or life more abundant, for the German people. Its purpose was exclusively to make Germany invincible by protecting her against the danger of such a blockade as that experienced between 1914 and 1918. And finally on top of all this Hitler himself designed and insisted on the execution of grandiose schemes for rebuilding Germany. A vast net of automobile roads was laid out all over the country, most of them again primarily for military purposes. The principal cities, first of all Berlin and in second place Munich, the official capital of the National Socialist movement and headquarters of the party, but also Hamburg, Frankfort, and other places, were to be adorned by magnificient public buildings of all sorts.

Obviously, a nation that attacks such numerous and grandiose schemes all at the same time needs all its man-

The Third Reich

power and natural resources—and still will not have enough of either. This deficiency is of course aggravated by the permanent withdrawal from the labor market of about 1,500,000 young men for army duty and the unproductive employment of at least from 1,000,000 to 2,000,000 men in the service of the party, the police, and the supervisory organization essential to the functioning of a compulsory planned economy.

In order to achieve complete control over the economic resources of the country the Government had first to create a thorough and most comprehensive organization of the whole economic life—man power, material, transportation, distribution, capital, and credit.

AGRICULTURE

As early as the autumn of 1933 the whole agricultural sector of Germany's economic life was organized in the so-called Reichsnährstand (Reich's Food Estate). It was a sort of public, compulsory cartel including not only producers, landowners, and tenants of every size of holding, but also the processors and wholesale and retail distributors of agricultural products. In 1934 and 1935 most agricultural producers were organized in so-called Marktverbände (Marketing Boards, comparable to the code authorities of the defunct American NRA). Each of these Marktverbände was administered by Market Commissioners (Marktbeauftragte). These Markt-

243

German Economy

verbände had to fix prices, to regulate supplies, to prescribe permissible charges for the various phases of processing (for instance, how much the miller may charge for milling the grain, the baker for baking the flour, the retailer for selling the bread). Gradually, the regulation grew tighter and tighter, particularly for bread, butter, eggs, potatoes, wool, cattle, and hogs. For some of these products certain quantities were ordered for delivery by individual farmers, the processors were strictly bound to confine themselves to certain qualities, the sales of various products had to be made exclusively to and through the organization prescribed by the authorities. The farmer has to grow what he is ordered to grow, he has to use the type of seeds that are stipulated. He is told what sort and what quantity of fertilizer he must apply. He is under strict supervision with respect to his technical methods, and so on and so forth.

As the prices the farmer received were relatively satisfactory—they were entirely independent of the world market and kept immune against fluctuations, and Germany had a sequence of several good crops—the farmer was relatively well off. Nevertheless, Germany had not come nearer the goal of self-sufficiency in food which this whole policy was destined to achieve. As a matter of fact, agricultural production since 1933 has hardly risen at all.

The Third Reich

TABLE 14

Agricultural Production

(thousands of tons)

	1933	1936	1937	1938
Wheat	5,765	4,523	4,576	5,502
Rye	8,727	7,386	6,917	8,463
Oat	6,952	5,618	5,919	6,274
Barley	3,468	3,399	3,638	4,177
Potatoes	44,071	46,324	55,310	50,903
Sugar beets	8,582	12,096	15,701	14,966

As is seen from Table 14, real progress has been made only with potatoes and sugar beets. The latter were particularly favored as a substitute for fats. Imports of various grains have risen. The import figures, however, are not quite conclusive, as a substantial part of imported foodstuffs has undoubtedly been stored as a war reserve. Nor is the picture presented by meat and dairy production more satisfactory. The number of hogs actually declined from 24,180,000 in 1932 to 23,410,000 in 1938. Milk production between 1932 and 1938 rose from 24,700,000 to 25,400,000 metric tons, butter production during the same period rose from 448,000 to 560,000 tons, and this increase was made exclusively through imported fodder. In fats there is still the gravest shortage in Germany's food supply. Despite the substantial imports of fodder stuffs of all sorts, Germany's imports of fats could hardly be reduced during the six years of National Socialism. Germany is still

German Economy

dependent on imports for nearly half of her consumption of fats, although German fat consumption is very moderate if measured by American standards. This result is the more remarkable because every year German agriculture has spent steadily increasing amounts for new machinery and equipment, and the prices of fertilizer were substantially reduced by government decree in order to increase its consumption. Other subsidies to agriculture were granted by means of reductions in taxes and interest. For example, during the last five years taxes paid by the farmers were reduced 60,000,000 marks, interest charges, 280,000,000 marks. And finally, the farmers were assigned cheap labor, particularly during harvesttime, through the various youth organizations of the party.

INDUSTRY AND TRADE

The organization of industry and trade is not less comprehensive than that of the agricultural sector. The fundamental law for business is the Law for Preparation of the Organic Constitution of the German Economy of February 27, 1934. It is the German form of the corporate state erected in Italy, but very different in its organization and its purpose. While it is to some extent the realization of the old, although vague, idea of a state of estates, it has nothing to do with self-government or the relation between capital and labor. The law author-

246

The Third Reich

izes the Minister of Economics to recognize trade organizations as the sole representative of their branch, to organize, dissolve, or merge trade associations, to change and supplement bylaws and charters, to appoint and recall the leaders, and so on. The former Chambers of Commerce, which in Germany were public bodies and had substantial administrative functions on the principle of self-government, were subjected to the so-called leadership principle, the leaders being appointed by the Government.

The whole economy is organized in a twofold way, first by branches, second by regions. The main groups are industry, handicrafts, commerce, banks, insurance, and power. These main groups are again subdivided into various sections and subsections. The territorial organization divides business into districts that coincide with the districts for the "Labor Trustees." Each group has a leader who is appointed by the Government and who is absolute within his jurisdiction. The leader of a group may appoint members of his group to advisory councils.

It is altogether an extremely complicated organization, which includes without any exception everybody in business, and makes them subject to all the decrees, regulations, and controls the Government sees fit to order. There is no escape from this organization, the purposes of which have been described in a decree of the Minister of Economics of July, 1936. For example:

German Economy

"Technical instruction and enlightenment of members about new materials; economic instruction about market conditions of raw materials and semifinished products used by the various industries; suggestions for the improvement of production and management; advice on cartel questions; instruction on tax questions, freight rates, tariff policy, and questions of foreign exchange; promotion of research and training; treatment of questions of war economy, air-raid protection" . . . and so on.

Within the framework of this all-comprehensive organization every businessman is told what to produce, the methods of production to be applied, how much coal and raw materials he will be apportioned, which materials he may or may not use, the prices he must pay for the products he buys and the prices he may charge for the products he sells, from whom he may accept orders, to whom and through whom he may sell, the order in which he is to satisfy demands (for instance, sometimes government orders have the preference, sometimes export orders; among the government orders again, sometimes the army has to be satisfied first, sometimes the party).

The other groups are organized in a similar way. Behind every decree or suggestion stands, of course, the unlimited power of punishment both by the association itself and by the courts, or, where the courts are defective, by the secret police. For every important group of

The Third Reich

industry and trade there exists a so-called Ueberwach-ungsstelle (Control Office).

The basic condition for this system of planned economy is, of course, complete control over exports and imports. And this again is closely connected with the control of foreign exchange and capital supply. Not a single carload, not one parcel, can cross a German border in either direction without a special permit by the Government. No German is supposed to sell anything abroad without such a permit. Whether and when a permit is granted is not primarily a matter of market considerations. The German importer cannot buy where he gets the best quality at the lowest price. The German exporter cannot sell wherever he might find a competitive chance. An extremely elaborate system has been built up for the control of foreign exchange. Already in the spring of 1934 the Control Offices were authorized to fix quotas for purchases of raw materials and to limit inventories kept by manufacturers and dealers. A few months later the Reichsbank proceeded to a system of apportioning Devisen. This system was designed to secure the imports of raw materials necessary for armaments at the expense of raw materials required for civilian purposes. The Reichsbank created a scale of relative urgency differentiating between vital and nonvital imports. The vital imports were for armament purposes or food supplies for the population. But in order to maintain a certain amount of imports Ger-

German Economy

many had to export. Consequently, since exports must be maintained at any cost, a very complicated system of export subsidies, barter agreements, clearing agreements, and so on was gradually developed. It became increasingly important when the second Four Year Plan, proclaimed in 1937, established the goal, and held out the promise, of making Germany more or less self-sufficient in basic raw materials, particularly in case of war. The purpose and the effect of this rigid control of foreign trade have been a complete severance of any connection between domestic and foreign prices. As there is virtually no free competition either within Germany or between Germany and foreign countries, the price system does not function. As far as the domestic price level is concerned, the complete and rigid price control is necessary in order to prevent inflation. And as far as exports are concerned, the Government pays subsidies on every export transaction that is deemed necessary to pay for necessary imports. In some cases these subsidies amount to 50 per cent of the value.

The so-called Second Four Year Plan was announced by Adolf Hitler in the following words at the Nuremberg party rally of September, 1936:

Within four years Germany shall be independent from all foreign countries in respect to all those materials which it can produce at home by means of German ingenuity, our mining, engineering, and chemical industries. When the process of rearmament has been completed, the labor now employed

The Third Reich

therein will be diverted into productive channels through the development of the great new German raw-material industry.

This program as well as the entire organization of National Socialist economy has its precedent in the war economy developed for the defense against the blockade from 1914 to 1918. At that time, and ever since, Germany was and has been bent upon developing substitute materials. The scientific and technical problems of their production were solved long before National Socialism came into power. The difficulty was merely the economic application of scientific devices on a large scale. This difficulty consisted first in the huge amounts of capital that had to be diverted to the new plants from other purposes, where they were employed more economically. The second difficulty was that these new materials were several times as expensive as the materials they were supposed to replace. For example, the price of Buna (synthetic rubber) is about seven times the price of genuine rubber. The price differences between synthetic oil and textile fibers and the corresponding natural products are slightly less, but would still be forbidding in a free economy that has to adjust costs to prices offered by the market. In a closed militarized economy like the German these considerations do not matter, because the economic viewpoint is entirely subordinate to the military viewpoint.

Nevertheless, substantial progress has been made with respect to quantity, quality, and costs of substitute pro-

251

German Economy

duction. But toward the essential goal of becoming entirely self-sufficient and independent of foreign supplies Germany has not made much progress. It may be estimated that of the textile material required in peacetime about 40 per cent is covered by domestic production. Among natural materials, the greatest progress has been achieved in flax-growing, by heavy subsidies and a very high fixed price. Wool production has not been substantially increased. Of substitute materials the most important is staple fiber (*Zellwolle*) made from cellulose, and artificial silk (rayon and acetate). Both are dependent upon a sufficient supply of cellulose and therefore limited by the supply of woods, which, for various purposes, is already strained to the limit. Synthetic rubber, a product of lime and coal, came into mass production only in 1939. Motor oil gained from coal by hydrogenation and synthesis is produced in increasing volume. But both genuine oil from German wells and synthetic oil covered only about one-third of the peacetime demand. Wartime demand is, of course, several times higher.

Apart from the development of substitute materials, Germany is making every effort to develop her own resources of raw materials, irrespective of costs. We have mentioned oil and flax; we may add, as even more important and more needed, iron ore, copper, and zinc. But there again success so far has not been spectacular. Particularly for iron ore, Germany remains dependent

The Third Reich

for more than two-thirds of her consumption upon foreign supply, primarily from Sweden (which provides about 60 per cent of Germany's ore imports).

METHODS OF FOREIGN TRADE

Clearing agreements. A clearing agreement provides for a central clearing office to which the importer pays the amounts due to the foreign countries from which he buys. From these amounts due the clearing office pays national creditors and exporters to the debtor country. In other words, the importer of German goods, say in Switzerland, does not pay his German supplier but, through the clearing office, pays a Swiss national who has exported to Germany. The purpose and effect of these clearing agreements is to equalize the balance of payment between two countries that are partners to such an agreement. In several instances where Germany has an export surplus and at the same time must pay interest on foreign investments or other debts, the clearing is used to satisfy not only the exporter but also to a certain extent bondholders and other creditors. Such clearing agreements have been arranged between Germany and all important creditor countries except Great Britain and the United States.

Barter agreements. These are agreements between two countries to exchange a certain quantity of one kind of goods for a certain quantity of another, as, for

German Economy

instance, Brazilian coffee for German locomotives, Mexican oil for German pipes or drilling equipment, Turkish tobacco for German automobiles and typewriters.

Only a very small and steadily declining part of German foreign trade is carried on outside the framework of such regulating agreements among governments, implemented by private deals that in each individual case depend on a permit from the Government. Thereby the foreign trade of Germany has become a wholly political matter, and has been treated as such for years. The increasing power of the Reich was consciously and openly put behind every commercial treaty and every substantial private transaction in which German interests were involved abroad.

Despite every effort to increase Germany's foreign trade, little progress has been made in the last six years,

TABLE 15
German Foreign Trade
(reichsmarks)

	Imports	Exports	Difference
1928	13,769,000,000	11,851,000,000	—1,918,000,000
1929	13,245,000,000	13,042,000,000	— 203,000,000
1933	4,146,000,000	4,751,000,000	+ 605,000,000
1934	4,385,000,000	4,060,000,000	— 325,000,000
1935	4,088,000,000	4,162,000,000	+ 74,000,000
1936	4,141,000,000	4,660,000,000	+ 519,000,000
1937	4,375,000,000	4,788,000,000	+ 413,000,000
1938*	6,052,000,000	5,619,000,000	— 433,000,000

* Greater Germany (including Austria, but without the Sudetenland).

The Third Reich

both imports and exports remaining at a level of about one-third of those of 1928-29 (Table 15). Even for the years in which there was a slight surplus it must be remembered that this surplus did not mean an increase in gold or foreign exchange. Whatever surplus could be achieved in foreign trade was needed to pay a part of the foreign debt service wherever the purchasing countries had the power to withhold for this purpose the balance in their trade with Germany. And this was virtually true of all European creditor countries. As a result the emphasis of Germany's foreign trade shifted more and more to countries that live under a similar trade system, particularly those of southeastern Europe, while trade with western Europe lagged. Substantial progress has also been made in German trade with Latin American countries, although there Germany has only about regained her prewar position.

3. FINANCIAL POLICY

When the National Socialist regime embarked on an armament program of ever growing dimensions, its principal problem was supposed to be how to get the money for its limitless plans. Many inside and outside Germany were convinced that within a short time National Socialist policies were bound to end in bankruptcy and to be submerged by another great flood of inflation such as that experienced in the early 1920's.

German Economy

But year after year passed and no sign of immediate financial weakness or imminent threat of uncontrolled inflation became visible. Was it a miracle? Were the men who devised and conducted this policy magicians, as they were depicted in so many newspaper and magazine articles? As a matter of fact, there is nothing miraculous about the German achievements of the last five years as far as economics and finance are concerned, and there is not even much essentially new in the chief features of this policy.

When a government has complete control over the man power and the material resources of a country, the only limit to the expansion of production is precisely this man power and these natural resources. Men have to be fed, housed, and clad, but the quantity and quality of food, shelter, and clothing are subject to wide variation. Science will tell you that the average human being requires 2,500 calories for the maintenance of his physical substance. In a free capitalist country the individual is at liberty to eat more if he can pay for it, and to compose his diet in accordance with his tastes, and the markets supply him with everything he wants. In a dictatorship, men can eat only as much as, and only such foodstuffs as, the Government is willing and able to permit them. As far as production is concerned, in a free capitalist system what is being produced depends on price and capital supply. If more automobiles are demanded, production is adapted to the increased demand, which

The Third Reich

means that more steel, leather, glass, copper, cotton, and other materials go into automobiles. If more houses are wanted, and people are ready to pay for them, more bricks, cement, steel, lumber, go into construction. If people are willing to spend a greater part of their income for beauty or amusement, more capital is invested in beauty parlors, drugstores, night clubs, and movie theaters, which means again diverting steel, glass, lumber, copper, and labor into another field of activity. Labor and capital are directed into those channels which promise the highest profits, and withdrawn from other uses which yield no or inadequate profits. This is roughly the free play of the dynamics of the capitalist system.

In a totalitarian system it is not the free individual, not the consumer, who by his free decision determines the employment of labor and capital, but it is the Government that decides for what purposes, to what extent, and by what methods the human and material resources of the nation are to be employed, and the Government is not motivated by considerations of profit, but usually by considerations of a noneconomic nature. The predominant motives for the economic policy of the German Government have been to make Germany militarily the most powerful nation and a nation as independent as possible of foreign supplies.

In what ways can a government direct the economic resources of a nation into the desired channels? Prin-

257

German Economy

cipally, either by direct command over labor and materials or by the more indirect means of taxation, credit policy, price- and wage-fixing. The National Socialist Government has employed all these methods at the same time. Exactly to what extent, it is impossible to ascertain, because the National Socialist Government from the beginning did away with what has been considered in the modern world fundamental publicity about governmental actions—it suppressed the publication of the annual budget of government receipts and expenditures. About essential features of the National Socialist policy the historian, so far, must depend on guesswork. We do not know how much this government actually spent every year, nor do we know what the national debt amounts to.

The financial policy of National Socialist Germany was not developed on a preconceived plan. Rather it was improvised, and its methods were modified as needs changed. One aim, however, has seemed to remain conscious and unalterable from the beginning: the preservation of the purchasing power of the mark. The Government realized very early that with rapidly growing deficits, government expenditure, and credit expansion, nothing would prevent a rising tide of inflation if the purchasing power of the masses was allowed to grow with the money supply. Therefore the Government insisted from the very beginning on keeping wages and prices rigidly fixed. This did not preclude a rise in

The Third Reich

the income of the working class as a whole, because with rapidly expanding production more workers were employed, and those who were employed worked longer hours. But as at the same time the limited supply of materials and productive capacity had to be reserved primarily for the military purposes of the nation, consumption had to be kept down. Therefore the production of consumer goods was expanded only on a very limited scale—at least much less than the production of capital goods. Whatever consumer income was left in excess of production of consumer goods had to be taken away either by increased taxation or by enforced savings.

FINANCIAL WINDFALLS

There were three additional sources of an extraordinary and nonrecurrent nature to be used by the Government. One was the virtual expropriation of foreign creditors. The second was the seizure, in 1938 and early 1939, of Austrian and Czechoslovakian gold and foreign exchange. The third was confiscation of Jewish property.

As was explained in the preceding chapter, Germany's prosperity between 1924 and 1929 was largely predicated on the inflow of enormous amounts of foreign capital, both long-term and short-term. In the five years between 1925 and 1929 the net import of capital by Germany averaged 2,600,000,000 reichsmarks annu-

German Economy

ally. Although a large part of foreign capital had to be used for reparation payments, a substantial amount was nevertheless accumulated, and also the service for interest and amortization was maintained. When the Nazis first came into power, they complied with their foreign obligations in a particularly punctilious way. In April, 1933, the Reichsbank repaid voluntarily a credit of 485,000,000 reichsmarks that had been advanced to it during the banking crisis of June, 1931, by the central banks of England and France and the Bank for International Settlements. Thereby the Reichsbank reduced voluntarily its holdings of gold and foreign exchange from 920,000,000 reichsmarks as of the end of 1932, to 511,000,000 as of the end of April, 1933. It was obvious that the Government wished to demonstrate to the world both its willingness and its inability to continue payments. Already a few weeks later, in May, 1933, a transfer moratorium was declared as of July 1, 1933. Initially the Dawes Loan and the interest on the Young Loan were exempted from the moratorium. On other medium and long-term debts only a partial moratorium was declared. The German debtors were supposed to make their payments in favor of foreign creditors in reichsmarks paid into a special Conversion Fund at the Reichsbank. One half of this amount was to be transferred in cash up to the end of 1933. For the other half scrip certificates were issued. These scrips could be sold to the Golddiskontbank (a subsidiary

The Third Reich

of the Reichsbank) at one-half their face value. This was then about the value of the blocked mark. Apart from the reparation loans, the Swiss and the Dutch loans were exempted and satisfied fully, because Holland and Switzerland threatened to satisfy themselves by retention of a corresponding part from the proceeds of German exports. A few months later, in December, 1933, the cash transfer was reduced to 30 per cent of the interest (and nothing on capital maturities). And finally, in June, 1934, the transfer was completely suspended where no special agreements with individual countries provided for exceptions. From then on, as a rule, interest and repayment of capital to foreign countries were paid in blocked marks, which depreciated steadily and rapidly.

At the same time, when these various steps were taken the Reichsbank insisted on a demonstrative decline of its holdings of gold and foreign exchange. By June, 1934, these holdings had dropped to the trifle of 77,000,000 reichsmarks, and have remained officially at this level ever since. But apart from this official gold there were always secret reserves of gold and foreign exchange hidden under various accounts. These secret reserves were temporarily enlarged by the annexation of Austria in March, 1938, when the gold and foreign exchange of the Austrian National Bank (which was in good shape) were transferred to the Reichsbank, and

261

German Economy

one year later, by the incorporation of Czechoslovakia (March, 1939).

The refusal to transfer interest and capital to foreign creditors amounts to a compulsory investment in Germany of money that would otherwise have been legitimately withdrawn. The exact amount of this enforced contribution of foreigners to the German economy is not known, but it amounts to many million marks a year.

While this is permanent relief, unless Germany is one day obliged to resume payments, the confiscation of the gold and foreign exchange of the Austrian and the Czechoslovak central banks and the confiscation of Jewish property are of course only one-time benefits. The first relieved substantially the strain the otherwise unfavorable balance of trade imposed on Germany in 1938, and permitted her to maintain imports of foodstuffs and raw materials in a larger volume than would have been possible otherwise. About the value of confiscated Jewish property nothing has been published, and even an estimate is made impossible by the wholly arbitrary valuation used in almost all cases. But it certainly amounts to several billion marks.

Expansion of economic activity in Germany since the ascendancy into power of the National Socialist regime is reflected by the increase in national income (Table 16).

The Third Reich

TABLE 16

German National Income

(reichsmarks)

1929	75,900,000,000
1932	45,200,000,000
1936	64,900,000,000
1937	71,000,000,000
1938	76,000,000,000*

* Without Austria and the Sudetenland. It is noteworthy that while Germany only in 1938 regained the national income of 1929, the national income in England in 1937 already exceeded that of 1929 by almost 20 per cent.

The National Socialist party took over the government at the low point of the "Great Depression." During this depression the last Republican governments, fighting against rising deficits, had most unpopularly increased taxes to a very high level. The National Socialist government, contrary to all promises, not only did not reduce these taxes but increased some of them and added others. The effect was a rapid increase in tax receipts, as is shown in Table 17.

TABLE 17

Total Receipts from German Taxes and Custom Duties

(reichsmarks)

1928-29	9,023,000,000
1932-33	6,647,000,000
1935-36	9,654,000,000
1937-38	13,964,000,000
1938-39	17,000,000,000 *

* Estimate

263

German Economy

Thus the income of the Reich from taxation (not including taxes of the states and municipalities of about 5,000,000,000 reichsmarks) was more than doubled within five years. But this was by no means sufficient to cover the actual expenditure. The best estimate is that at the same time the national debt rose from 11,700,-000,000 reichsmarks at the end of the fiscal year 1932-33 to about 40,000,000,000 or 45,000,000,000 by the end of 1938, of which about 15,000,000,000 or 20,000,-000,000 are "secret," that is, not shown in the official statements of the Treasury—chiefly technically short-term bills held in the portfolios of industrial corporations or various banks. Taxation proper altogether amounts to about 30 per cent of the national income, to which must be added several billion reichsmarks, or another 5 per cent to 10 per cent, for social-security taxes and more or less "voluntary" contributions for various party purposes.

4. THE SOCIAL STRUCTURE UNDER NATIONAL SOCIALISM

National Socialism came into power under the pretense of creating an entirely new social order. We have cited a few passages in the party program that refer to this new social order. What actually was done in 1933 and 1934 was not even hinted at in the party program. Having grown and come into power through the fight

The Third Reich

against "Marxism," which was identified with the idea of the class struggle, National Socialism from the beginning bent every effort to break the spirit of the class struggle and to substitute for it the ideal of race and a people's community (*Volksgemeinschaft*).

Only seven weeks after the elections of March 5, 1933, which definitely established the National Socialist dictatorship, Dr. Goebbels, Minister of Propaganda, announced on April 24 in a proclamation that

the government of the National Revolution has decided to make the First of May a holiday of national labor. . . . We have become a poor people, but nobody can deprive us of the joyful will to live, of the courage for work, of the intrepid optimism that overcomes all obstacles. The whole people honor themselves by giving labor the honor that it deserves. Germans of all ranks, groups, and vocations join hand with one another. United we march into the new epoch.

May 1, 1933, was celebrated throughout the Reich with all the magnificence and splendor, all the impressive stage setting, for which National Socialism has since established its reputation. May 1, which for many years had been celebrated by the Socialist parties and unions as a holiday of protest against the existing order, was suddenly converted into a holiday of allegiance to the new political system. With the workers the great industrialists, chairmen and presidents of the biggest corporations, had to march in the same lines, and sometimes not in the van but in the rear. The impression was enormous.

German Economy

On May 2, 1933, all offices of all unions in Germany were seized by Storm Troopers, their leaders and officers were arrested, maltreated, or sent to concentration camps, their property was confiscated. The autonomous organizations of German labor, built up over several decades and enormously strengthened, particularly in the fifteen years of Republican regime, were destroyed in one day. They were inherited by the German Labor Front. This Labor Front was no longer an organization of workers. It was a section of the National Socialist party, and included not only workers and employees but also all entrepreneurs and professional men.

The legal basis for this revolutionary step was not created until January, 1934, when the Law to Regulate National Labor, pretentiously called the Magna Carta of German labor, was issued. Until the emergency decrees of the Brüning Cabinet, free collective bargaining between trade-unions and associations of industry was considered the normal, desirable way of regulating wages. Arbitration by the Government was permissible only when negotiations between unions and employers had failed. Strikes and lockouts were legal as long as and as far as no collective contract had been achieved, and illegal strikes and lockouts were not criminal offenses but were merely subject to private damage claims. By the emergency decrees of Brüning, for the first time wages could be fixed by the dictate of the Government without preceding negotiations between unions and em-

The Third Reich

ployers. What was meant as an emergency measure by the Brüning government was made a permanent principle by the National Socialist regime. The task of regulating wages and labor conditions was assigned to the Labor Front, which appointed so-called Labor Trustees (*Treuhänder der Arbeit*), who constituted the highest authorities in all labor disputes. There are fourteen Labor Trustees, according to the division of the party organization into fourteen districts (*Gaue*). These trustees are civil servants of the Ministry of Labor, from which they receive their instructions. The old shop council was preserved, though the name was changed to "council of confidence" (*Vertrauensrat*). But it had to be elected exclusively from a panel to be made up by the employer, now called the "shop leader," together with the National Socialist "shop cell" (*Betriebszelle*), which represented the party. These elections were held only twice, and were suspended after 1935. Since then the spokesman of the employees in every shop or factory has been virtually the leader of the party cell, and it is a question of personality and accident whether he or the employer has the greater pull with the party authorities and therefore the decisive voice. Since 1933 changes in wage rates have been forbidden as a matter of principle, and the length of working time is prescribed by the Labor Front. Consequently, this whole mechanism is devoted to decisions on frictions as they result in daily life.

German Economy

But apart from regulating wages and hours, the Labor Front has assumed great new tasks with which the former unions never were, nor could be, concerned. The law of 1934 established an important new ideology. It set up Social Honor Courts to judge "gross violations of social duties." Under this phrase are understood "misuse of authority and willful and malicious exploitation of the followers [the term now used for employees corollary to "leader" for the employer] or offenses against their honor by an owner of an establishment or the leader of the establishment or their representatives." Such an employer or his substitute may be sentenced to heavy fines or even to disqualification as leader of an establishment, that is, he may be excluded from the management of his property. On the other hand, employees may be prosecuted for "willful and malicious agitation among the followers such as to endanger in-dustrial peace or disturbance of the community spirit in the establishment." That may mean practically that any expression of discontent may be penalized by dismissal and subsequent starvation.

But above all, the Labor Front is an enormous propaganda organization. Besides "Honor of Work," it must achieve and safeguard "Beauty of Work." This latter division of the Labor Front "deals with questions such as improvement of ventilation and light in factories, installation of rest rooms, improvement in the standard of working-conditions from an esthetic point of view

The Third Reich

by voluntary schemes, such as garden plots in the factories, removal of junk heaps, and so forth." Under pressure from the Labor Front hundreds of millions of marks are being spent annually by industry for such schemes.

But the most important part of the activities of the Labor Front is the organization "Strength through Joy" (*Kraft durch Freude*). It is a tremendous endeavor to organize collectively the leisure of the people. Men must not be left to themselves. The totalitarian state does not admit of a real private life. Therefore even the recreation after working hours must be organized and supervised by the party, directed into channels that lead to the aggrandizement of the power of the party over men. "Strength through Joy" provides vacation travel, theater performances, courses in gymnastics, and all sorts of sports, lectures and courses in the arts, and so on. The Labor Front has built or chartered its own vacation steamers, has built or bought huge hotels at the best seaside and mountain resorts, has hired special trains and autobus fleets for its members, and all this at extremely low prices within the income of every employee. Some of these enterprises are subsidized, but most are self-supporting because the costs are greatly reduced by the mass participation. The means at the disposal of the Labor Front run into several hundred million marks a year. They are raised by a tax of no less than 1.5 per cent on all wages and salaries—this in addition to a 6 per

German Economy

cent wage tax for the unemployment fund, although there is no unemployment any longer, besides the contributions to the other branches of social insurance. One may estimate that the average worker has to pay about 30 per cent of his wage income in taxes and contributions of this sort.

All the social achievements of the Weimar Republic have been maintained or even extended under the National Socialist regime. At the same time, unemployment has been abolished; it is replaced by an increasing shortage of labor. The income of the working class as a whole has risen (although hourly wages have remained unchanged and their real purchasing power has been diminished). But workers and salaried persons have to pay their price for this in the loss of political freedom in general, and especially their freedom of movement. In a growing number of industries, if workers are dissatisfied they cannot leave their jobs without the consent of the authorities. If they do, they are not permitted to find employment anywhere else or to receive relief. Every worker is supplied with a workbook that tells the story of his employment. A black mark in such a workbook amounts to a death sentence. While the position of labor as a class has undoubtedly been improved, the status of an individual worker or employee has virtually degenerated to serfdom. At the same time no worker can be arbitrarily dismissed by the employer, though his party boss can dismiss him any time for

The Third Reich

real or alleged political reasons. Labor is apportioned to industry in the same way and on the same principle as raw materials. And of course the Government has the first choice for its own purposes. Therefore, for instance, every worker can be ordered for fortification work or road-building at any time to any part of the country. His family, left behind, is taken care of at fixed low rates.

5. SUMMARY AND OUTLOOK

By the end of 1938 Germany had reached the crucial point of her economic expansion—the point where the last reserves in man power, material, and productive capacity had been utilized in the service of the most ambitious power politics ever adopted by any government in modern times. The economic or financial collapse so many had heralded years before had not occurred, and in theory it did not need to occur had peace been preserved. Germany has gradually developed an economic system sui generis that can be maintained indefinitely provided only the Government refrains from exaggerating its adventure and the people remain ready to endure a complete deprivation of individual liberty. The survival of the present German system offers no insuperable financial problem. A government that completely controls (by the most comprehensive terror system) foreign trade, domestic consumption,

German Economy

costs of production, and domestic investments is always able to procure the financial means for its purposes. And it is of secondary importance whether these means are raised by taxation, by short-term or long-term borrowing, or even by printing paper money. The danger point arises if and when a government undertakes to push expansion beyond the natural limits of available resources.

How real this danger was has been demonstrated to the world by the resignation of Dr. Schacht from the Reichsbank at the end of 1938. If, after full utilization of industrial capacity, more money is poured out by the Government, even the terror of the secret police is of no avail, because it would have to be directed against government agencies themselves, which would compete with one another for the available resources. If there is a limited amount of steel, it has to be used primarily for armament, for railroad equipment, or for party buildings. But if money is being appropriated for all these purposes at one and the same time beyond the supply of steel, inflationist effects are bound to develop. On the other hand, there may perhaps be no rigid limitation of available labor. It may be possible to increase labor efficiency by technical improvements or by greater employment of women or by prolonging working hours. But if labor is exploited beyond a certain limit, labor efficiency will decrease, not increase. For this reason, for example, coal production in Germany had

The Third Reich

already begun to decline because production per man and shift was falling off. For the same reason, the quality of production had begun to deteriorate. This in itself again endangered Germany's precarious position in foreign markets, which must be maintained at almost any cost.

And the incentives to push ahead along the lines pursued in the last few years were enhanced by the armament race the Western Powers had begun to enter upon. Their advantage in this race was enormous. They started with huge unused reserves against a Germany that already showed every sign of utmost strain. And they could save all the billions Germany spent on plants for the production of expensive substitute materials by being able to buy cheap natural materials.

But there was nothing intrinsic in the German economic system that would have required its use exclusively or primarily for armament and other unproductive purposes and its subordination to these purposes of the standard of living of the people. It is easily conceivable that the same methods could be employed for peaceful purposes, that residences would be built instead of fortifications, automobiles instead of tanks, fertilizer made instead of gunpowder, and finally exports used for buying butter instead of material for guns. A peaceful Germany could always have found outlets for its products, as it had done in pre-Hitler days.

What was and still is at stake is political, not eco-

German Economy

nomic, issues. Political issues in Germany itself: How long will the German people bear the strain imposed on it by the most ruthless dictatorship, by police terror, corruption, and exploitation for the major glory not only of the German Reich but of the ruling group that treats the German people as its private property? Political issues in the world at large: Will the world bear the strain of nerves under which Germany had forced it to live for several years by a perpetual threat of war?

The answer to the second question was given on September 3, 1939, when Great Britain and France took up arms to destroy Hitlerism. The answer to the first question is yet to be given. It will depend on victory or defeat.

BIBLIOGRAPHY

BIBLIOGRAPHY

Prewar Period

GENERAL

BOWDEN, WITT, and others, *An Economic History of Europe since 1750.* New York, 1937.

BRUCK, WERNER FRIEDRICH, *Social and Economic History of Germany.* London, 1938.

CLAPHAM, J. H., *The Economic Development of France and Germany, 1815–1914.* Cambridge, 1936.

DAWSON, WILLIAM H., *Bismarck and State Socialism.* London, 1890.

—— *The Evolution of Modern Germany.* New York, 1908.

HOWARD, EARL DEAN, *The Cause and Extent of the Recent Industrial Progress of Germany.* Boston, 1907.

KNOWLES, L. C. A., *Economic Development in the Nineteenth Century, France, Germany, Russia and the United States.* London, 1932.

SOMBART, WERNER, *The German National Economy in the 19th Century.* Berlin, 1903.

VEBLEN, THORSTEIN, *Imperial Germany and the Industrial Revolution.* New York, 1915.

WALTERSHAUSEN, FREIHERR AUGUST SARTORIUS VON, *The History of German Economy, 1815–1914.* Jena, 1920.

BANKS AND CURRENCY

FLINK, SALOMON, *The German Reichsbank and Ecqnomic Germany (with special reference to the period after 1923).* New York, 1930.

Bibliography

JOSEPH, LEOPOLD, *The Evolution of German Banking.* London, 1913.

RIESSER, J., *The German Great Banks and Their Concentration in Connection with the Economic Development of Germany.* Washington, 1911.

SCHULZE-GAEVERNITZ, GERHART VON, *The German Credit Bank.* Tübingen, 1922.

UNITED STATES GOVERNMENT, NATIONAL MONETARY COMMISSION, *The Reichsbank.* Washington, 1910.

WHALE, P. BARRETT, *Joint Stock Banking in Germany.* London, 1930.

TRADE POLICY

DAWSON, WILLIAM HARBUTT, *Protection in Germany: A History of German Fiscal Policy during the 19th Century.* London, 1904.

COLONIAL POLICY

GIORDANI, PAOLO, *The German Colonial Empire, Its Beginning and Ending.* London, 1916.

TOWNSEND, MARY EVELYN, *The Rise and Fall of Germany's Colonial Empire, 1884–1918.* New York, 1930.

CARTELS AND TRUSTS

LIEFMAN, ROBERT, *Cartels, Concerns and Trusts.* London, 1932.

——— *International Cartels, Combines and Trusts.* London, 1927.

PRIBRAM, KARL, *Cartel Problems,* Washington, 1933.

TRADE UNIONISM

SANDERS, WILLIAM STEPHEN, *Trade Unionism in Germany.* London, 1916.

Bibliography

Seidel, Richard, *The Trade Union Movement of Germany*. Amsterdam, 1928. International Trade Union Library, Nos. 7–8.

War Period

GENERAL

Bruck, Werner Friedrich, *Social and Economic History of Germany*. London 1938.

Mendelssohn-Bartholdy, Albrecht, *The War and German Society: The Testament of a Liberal*. New Haven, 1937. Economic and Social History of the World War, German Series.

WAR FINANCES

Flink, Salomon, *The German Reichsbank and Economic Germany*. New York, 1930.

Lotz, Walther, *The Financial Policy of the German Government during the War*. New Haven, 1927. Economic and Social History of the World War, German Series.

WAR EMERGENCY ECONOMY

Goebel, O. H., *German Raw Material Economy in the World War*. New Haven, 1930. Economic and Social History of the World War, German Series.

Skalweit, A. K. F., *The German War Food Policy*. New Haven, 1927. Economic and Social History of the World War, German Series.

LABOR RELATIONS

Umbreit, Paul, *The War and Labor Conditions: The German Trade Unions during the War*. New Haven,

Bibliography

1928. Economic and Social History of the World War, German Series.

Weimar Period

GENERAL

ANGELL, JAMES W., *The Recovery of Germany*. New Haven, 1932.

BOWDEN, WITT, and others, *An Economic History of Europe since 1750*. New York, 1937.

BRUCK, WERNER FRIEDRICH, *Social and Economic History of Germany*. London, 1938.

ROLL, ERICH, *Spotlight on Germany: A Survey of Her Economic and Political Problems*. London, 1933.

SCHMIDT, CARL T., *German Business Cycles, 1924–1933*. New York, 1934.

REPARATIONS

BERGMANN, KARL, *The History of Reparations*. Boston, 1927.

DAWSON, SIR PHILIPP, *Germany's Industrial Revival*. London, 1926.

KEYNES, JOHN MAYNARD, *The Economic Consequences of the Peace*. London, 1920.

McFADYEAN, SIR ANDREW, *Reparation Reviewed*. London, 1930.

MOULTON, HAROLD G. AND CONSTANTINE E. McGUIRE, *Germany's Capacity to Pay*. New York, 1923.

SCHACHT, HJALMAR, *The End of Reparations: The Economic Consequences of the World War*. New York, 1931.

SERING, MAX, *Germany under the Dawes Plan: Origin,*

Bibliography

Legal Foundations and Economic Effects of the Reparation Payments. London, 1929.

INFLATION PERIOD

DAWSON, SIR PHILIPP, *Germany's Industrial Revival.* London, 1926.

PRICE, MORGAN P., *Germany in Transition.* London, 1923.

SCHACHT, HJALMAR, *The Stabilization of the Mark.* London, 1927.

PROSPERITY

BRADY, ROBERT A., *The Rationalisation Movement in German Industry.* London, 1933.

MEAKIN, WALTER, *The New Industrial Revolution.* New York, 1928.

MONETARY POLICY

FLINK, SALOMON, *The German Reichsbank and Economic Germany.* New York, 1930.

AGRICULTURAL POLICY

HOLT, JOHN BRADSHAM, *German Agricultural Policy 1918–1934: The Development of a National Philosophy in Post-War Germany.* Chapel Hill, N. C., 1936.

CARTELS AND TRUSTS

LEVY, HERMANN, *Industrial Germany: A Study of Its Monopoly Organizations and Their Control by the State.* Cambridge, 1935.

MICHELS, RUDOLF, *Cartels, Combines and Trusts in Post-War Germany.* New York, 1928.

PRIBRAM, KARL, *Cartel Problems.* Washington, 1933.

Bibliography

STOCKDER, ARCHIBALD H., *German Trade Associations: The Coal Cartels*. New York, 1924.

STOCKING, GEORGE WARD, *The Potash Industry: A Study in State Control*. New York, 1931.

WARRINER, D., *Combines and Rationalisation in Germany*. London, 1928.

LABOR RELATIONS

GUILLEBAUD, C. W., *The Works Council: A German Experiment in Industrial Democracy*. Cambridge, 1928.

REICH, NATHAN, *Labor Relations in Republican Germany: An Experiment in Industrial Democracy, 1918–1933*. New York, 1938.

SEIDEL, RICHARD, *The Trade Union Movement of Germany*. Amsterdam, 1928. International Trade Union Library, Nos. 7–8.

STERN, BORIS, *Works Council Movement in Germany*. Washington, 1925. U. S. Bureau of Labor Statistics, Bulletin No. 383.

Hitler Period

ASCOLI, MAX, AND FEILER, ARTHUR, *Fascism for Whom?* London, 1939.

BALOGH, THOMAS, "The National Economy of Germany," *Economic Journal*, September, 1938.

BRUCK, WERNER FRIEDRICH, *Social and Economic History of Germany*. London, 1938.

HEIDEN, CONRAD, *History of National Socialism*. London, 1937.

HITLER, ADOLF, *Mein Kampf*. Unexpurgated edition. London, 1939.

Bibliography

SCHUMAN, FREDERICK L., *The Nazi Dictatorship*. London, 1936.

STERNBERG, FRITZ, *Germany and a Lightning War*. London, 1938.

INDEX

INDEX

Acreage, 37
Adriatic, 5
Advisory Board for Municipal
    Credits, 188
A.E.G., *see* General Electric
Africa, 68
Agriculture, 23, 25, 26, 34, 36, 41,
    44, 63, 64, 77, 92, 111, 112, 114,
    116, 120, 182-185, 210
    credits, 206, 210
    duties, 62, 65
    prices, 243-246
    subsidies, 246
Allgemeiner Deutscher Gewerk-
    schaftsbund, 90
Allies, xiii, xiv, xvii, xviii, 15, 59,
    108, 109, 126, 130, 170, 172, 175,
    178, 273
Alps, 5, 6
Alsace-Lorraine, xvii, xviii, 24, 30,
    34, 35, 41, 63, 72, 135, 136
Amalgamations, 50
America, *see* United States of
    America
Aluminium, 208
Anatolian Railroad Co., 59, 105
Anderson, Marta, xx
Anglo-Saxon, 76, 85, 88
Ankara, 59
Anticapitalism, *see* Capitalism
Anti-Socialist Laws, 66, 78-80, 90,
    121
Anti-Trust Laws, 83
Arbitration, 266
Archduke, Austrian, 14
Armament, 42, 60, 95, 120, 128, 130,
    136, 239, 241, 249, 273
Army, 13, 29, 84, 116, 126, 128, 183,
    221, 224, 243
Aryan race, 236

Asia Minor, 58, 60
Assignates, 164, 165
Austria, 5-8, 11, 14, 24, 26, 27, 54,
    59, 62, 66, 84, 188, 241, 261
Austria-Hungary, 14, 15, 24, 40, 58,
    59, 96, 97
Austrian Credit Anstalt, 188
Austrian National Bank, 261
Autarchy, 61, 66, 96, 108, 251, 252
Authoritarian, 12
Auxiliary Service, 119, 120, 124, 125

Bach, Johann Sebastian, 4, 8
Baden, 28, 71
Baden, Max von, 137
Baghdad, 59, 60
    Bahn, 60
Balance of payments, 35, 56, 137
Balkans, xv, 58
Ballin, Albert, 236
Baltic Sea, xviii, 67
Bamberger, Ludwig, 33
Banca Commerciale Italiana, 54
Banca Generala Romana, 55
Bank of England, 190
Bank of France, 190
Bank for International Settlements,
    174, 175, 198
Banknotes, 33, 97, 100, 107, 154
Banks, German (*see also* Reichs-
    bank), 19, 20, 25, 33, 44-51, 76
    capital, 186, 191
    crisis, 186-193
    holiday, 190
Banks of Issue, 31, 33, 45, 46, 76
    savings, 46, 77
Bardeckung, 99
Barter, 253-255
Bartholomew's Day, 116
Bavaria, 7, 28, 72

287

Index

Bebel, August, 89, 121
Beethoven, Ludwig van, 8
Belgium, xiv, xvi, xvii, 62, 68, 86
Berlin, 8, 18, 26, 49, 50, 77, 224, 225, 242
Berliner Handelsgesellschaft, 47, 191
Bernstein, Eduard, 79
Bethman-Hollweg, Theobald von, 13
Bills of Exchange Law, 27
Bismarck, Otto von, 11, 12, 15, 16, 23, 29, 30, 33, 61, 65-67, 73, 74, 78, 82, 92, 121, 146, 211
Blitzkrieg, xii, xiii
Blockade, xiv-xvii, 96, 109, 110, 251
Blocked Mark, 261
Bohemia, 6, 7, 24
Bolshevik, 18, 127-129
Booms, German, 35, 36, 47, 63, 157
Borsig Werke, 26
Bosnia, 14
Bourgeoisie, 9, 13
Brandenburg, Mark of, 7
Braunschweig, 71
Braunthal, Alfred, xx
Bremen, 24, 32, 67
    S.S., 178
British Empire, xiii, 15, 60
British Recovery Act, 141, 144
Brüning, Heinrich, 19, 185, 194, 196, 210, 220-222, 238, 266
"Building years," 36
Bülow, Prince von, 66
Buna, 251
Bund, German, 24, 29
    North German, 27, 29, 30, 74, 88
Bundesrat, 123
Business Control, see Industries, Control of

California, 25
Capital, "creative" and "rapacious," 236
    exports, 53-60, 69, 137
    foreign, 57, 58, 68, 162, 179-181, 188, 190, 206, 255, 259-262

issues, 45, 57
    levy, 31, 148
Capitalism, 10, 18, 77, 84, 85, 92, 110, 220, 232
Caprivi, Georg von, 66
Card System, see Rationing
Carolines, 68
Cartels, 51, 83-88, 209, 210
Catastrophes, German, 3, 16, 17
Catholic, 9, 89
Center Party, 89, 147, 221
Central Powers, 126
Charles V, 5
Chambers of Commerce, 247
Chemical industries, 26, 43, 44, 111, 177, 208, 209, 251, 252
China, 55, 68
Christian, 8
    Socialist, 78
    unions, 89, 90, 216
Circulation, 33, 97, 99, 100, 107, 154
Civil Code, 28
Civil Manager, 138
Civil Service, 195
Clearing, 253
Cobden Treaty, 62
Collapse, 17, 112, 129, 130
Collective Labor Contracts, 91, 212, 216
Collectivism, 84
Cologne, 46
Colonies, 29, 58, 60, 67, 69, 136
Commercial Code, 27
Commercialization, 175
Commercial Treaties, 62
Commerz & Discontbank, 50
Commerz & Privatbank, 50
Communists, 19, 29, 220, 222, 224, 230
Competition, free, 82-85
    cutthroat, 87
Compulsory Loan, 148
Concentration, 49-51, 86, 191
    camps, 13
Conciliation, 124
Conscription, xii, 120, 241
Conservatives, 13, 18

288

Index

Constantinople, 59
Consumers, 91, 112, 113, 123
Contributions, 81, 246
Control of state securities, 102
Coolidge, Calvin, 168
Co-operatives, 91, 92, 195
Cost of living, 37, 123
Councils, 198, 199
  of Confidence, 267
Crafts, 41, 82, 90
Credit Mobilier, 46
Crisis, see Depression
Currency, 18, 19, 25, 31-33, 35, 97,
  99, 103, 193, 261
Cuno, Wilhelm, 144
Customs, 24, 27, 29, 62, 63
Czarism, 127, 128
Czechoslavakia, 14, 241, 262

Danube, 5
Danzig, 67
Darlehenskassen, 99, 100
  -scheine, 99, 100
Darmstädter Bank, 47, 50, 51
  & Nationalbank, 190, 191, 236
Dawes, Charles C., 169
  Plan, 18, 139, 144, 145, 169-171,
    172, 175
  Loan, 140, 179, 180
Debt, public, 30, 45, 73, 149, 258,
  264
Deflation, 193-198
Delbrück, Adalbert von, 236
  Rudolf von, 33, 61, 65, 73
Democracy, 11, 13, 221
Denmark, xvi, 11, 15, 109
Demilitarized Zone, 242
Depression, 36, 63, 72, 85, 181-193
  world, 25, 36, 64, 193
Dernburg, Bernhard, 69
Deutsche Allgemeine Zeitung, 159
Deutsch-Asiatische Bank, 55
Deutsche Bank, 47, 49, 50, 51, 54,
  55, 59, 105, 236
  Bau-und Bodenbank, 205
Deutsche Golddiskontbank, 206,
  207

Deutsch Luxemburgische Berg-
  werksgesellschaft, 158, 159
Deutschnationale Volkspartei, 222
Deutsche Orientbank, 55
  Rentenbank, 166, 167, 206
  -Kreditanstalt, 206
Deutsch-Südamerikanische Bank, 55
Deutsche Überseebank, 55
  Volkspartei, 159
Diamonds, 69
Dictatorship (see also Part V),
  80, 129
Disconto-Gesellschaft, 47, 49-51,
  55, 236
Disarmament, 221
Dollar, 151-153
Drang nach dem Osten, 58
Dresdner Bank, 47, 50, 51, 55, 59,
  191
Dürer, Albrecht, 4
Dye Works, see I. G. Dye Works

Economy, free, 110, 111
Economic Ministry, 247
  warfare, xiv
Egypt, 55
Elbe, 5, 6
Elbia, East, 11
Electrical Industries, 43, 49, 177
  power, 43, 76, 203
Embargo, 112
Emergency Decrees, 196-198
Emigration, 39, 40, 68
Emperor, 13, 60, 75, 98
Empire, German (or Reich), 23-
  40, 44, 53, 62, 72, 106, 107, 122
Employees, 81, 82, 90, 120, 123,
  125, 212-218, 266-272
Employers, 81, 91, 120, 123-125,
  212, 266
Employment, 41, 43, 162
Engels, Friedrich, 80
England, 3, 4, 23-26, 32, 37, 40-46,
  52, 53, 60-64, 77, 84, 86, 88, 91,
  96, 109, 177, 223, 230, 243, 253,
  274

289

Index

Ersatz-stuffs, 113, 114, 242, 251, 252, 273
Erzberger, Matthias, 146, 147, 150
Essen, 26, 42
Essener Creditanstalt, 49
Europa, S.S., 178
Exchange, foreign, 107, 108, 137, 149-153, 168, 192, 249, 255, 260-262
  regulations, 192, 249, 260
Export subsidies, 250
Extremists, 196, 221

Farm, *see* Agriculture
Fats, xix, 113, 114, 245
Far East, 55
Feder, Gottfried, 238, 239
  Money, 238
Feudalism, 13, 20
Fichte, Johann Gottlieb, 10
Finances
  budget, 258
  expenditure, income, 101, 102, 105, 106
  mobilization, 96
  policy, 106, 107, 145-149, 255-264
  reform, 145-149
  sovereignty, 28, 29
  war, *see* War Financing
Flight from the Land, 40
Food, xix, 38, 53, 97, 109-112, 115, 116, 128, 245
  administration, war, 111
Foreign control, 172-174
  trade, xvi, 19, 38, 42, 43, 51-53, 60-66, 69, 137, 192-194, 210, 245, 250-255
Forestry, 41, 70, 77
Four Year Plans, xiii, 241, 242, 250, 251
Fourteen Points, 137
France, xvii, 3, 4, 8, 9, 11, 24, 25, 27, 32, 34, 35, 52, 56, 62, 66, 84, 86, 242, 274
Frankfort-on-Main, 46, 54, 242
  Peace Treaty of, 62
Frederick I, 7

Frederick II, 8, 16
Frederick William, Margrave, 7
Free Trade, 61
Free Unions, 89, 90, 120, 216
Fulfillment, Policy of, 180, 181
Fürth, 71

Galicia, 58
Gelsenkirchener Bergwerksgesell-schaft, 158, 159
General Electric Co., 43, 117, 173, 236
German Edison Co., 43
Gilchrist, 34
Glas, 86
Gilbert, Parker, 172
Goebbels, Paul Joseph, 265
Gold, 25, 32, 33, 97, 98, 100, 108, 189, 255, 260-262
  hoarding, 99
  mark, 148
  standard, 32, 35, 61, 98, 99
Government ownership, 70
Grain, 37, 38, 64-66, 109, 115, 116
Great Britain, *see* England
Guilds, 82, 83

Hallgarten & Co., 54
Hamburg, 24, 54, 67, 224, 242
Hamburg-Amerika-Packetfahrt-A. G. (Hapag), 236
Handel, George Frederick, 8
Hanover, 72
Hanoversche Bank, 49
Hanseatic League, 11
Hansemann, Adolf, 236
  Julius, 236
Hapsburg, 5-7, 14, 15
Haydn, Joseph, 8
Hegel, Georg Friedrich, 10
Helfferich, Karl, 105, 165
Hesse, 74
Herriot, Edouard, 169
Hilferding, Rudolf, 165
Hindenburg, Paul von, 183, 221, 224, 225
  Program, 119, 124

290

Index

Hirsch-Duncker Unions, 89, 90, 216
Hitler, Adolf, xi-xv, xviii, 3, 6, 12, 19, 20, 84, 96, 224, 225, 229, 234, 239, 241, 242
Hog Massacre, 114-116
Hohenzollern, 7
Holland, xiv, xvi, 17, 109, 261
Holy Roman Empire of the German Nation, 3, 5
Hoover, Herbert, 179
moratorium, 189, 193
Housing, 177, 203-205
Hugenberg, Alfred, 222, 241
Hughes, Charles Evans, 168
Hungary, 6, 64

I. G. Dye Works, 44, 209
Emigration, 40
Imperial Era, 75-77, 81
India, 55
Individualism, 11, 36, 38, 83
Industrialization, 23, 25, 34, 37, 40, 43, 44, 46, 48, 52, 56, 67, 77, 91, 111, 120
Industries, heavy, 25, 36, 40, 49, 63, 87, 112
Inflation, 3, 18, 46, 84, 99, 100, 104, 105, 108, 134, 162
Interallied debts, 173, 189
Interest reduction, compulsory, 196, 197, 238
Interest slavery, 233, 235-239
Interstate Commerce Commission, 74
Irma (International Railmakers Assn.), 86
Iron, xvii, xviii, 26, 34, 35, 41, 42, 62-65, 75, 85, 135, 252
Italy, xv, 6, 14, 40

Japan, 55
Jewish property, 262
Jewish race, 236
Jobbers & Heroes, 85
Joint stock companies, 36
Junkers, 9, 13, 65, 183-185

Kaiser, *see* Emperor
Kaiser, Wilhelm Canal, 67
Kapp, Friedrich, 149
Katheder-Socialismus, 87
Ketteler, Bishop, 78
Keynes, John Maynard, 23, 140
Kiaochow, 68, 69
Kleinwächter, Friedrich, 84
Kölner Bergwerksverein, 47
Königsberg, 67
Kriegsrohstoffabteilung, 117
Krupp, Friedrich, 26, 49, 112
Kuhn, Loeb & Co., 45

Labor, 39, 40, 83, 84, 110, 122, 175, 212-218, 247, 266-272
Front, 266-272
Ladenburg, Thalmann & Co., 54
Lansing, Robert, 138
Lassalle, Ferdinand, 89
Latin America, 55, 56, 58, 255
Lausanne Conference, 222, 223, 231
League of Nations, 231
"Lebensraum," 6
Leibnitz, Wilhelm, 4
Liberalism, xii, 11, 13, 18, 28, 32, 33, 60, 61, 70, 73, 76, 83, 84, 88, 110
Liebig, Justus von, 44, 64
Liebknecht, Wilhelm, 121
List, Friedrich von, 61
Loan banks, 99, 100
notes, 99, 107
Locarno Treaty, 242
London, 54, 80
Conference, 169
Ultimatum, 140, 150
Louis, XIV, 9
Ludendorff, Erich, 134
Luther, Hans, 165
Martin, 4, 6
Luxemburg, 26, 42

Macedonia, 59
Machines, 26, 42, 47, 62, 120, 177
Madrid, 6
Main, 5

291

Index

Maria Theresa, 8
Market Commissioner, 243
Marne, Battle on the, 96
Martial Law, 129
Marxism, 20, 232, 265
Matricular Contributions, 29, 30
Mecklenburg, 24
Mediation, 212-214
Mein Kampf, 231
Mercantilism, 70, 83, 84
Mercurbank, 54
Metric system, 28
Mevissen, Gustav von, 47, 236
Mexico, 56
Middle Ages, 3, 83
Middle class, 82, 92, 160, 233, 237
Military Law, 129
Mining, 34, 47, 75, 77, 86, 128, 129
Minoux, Friedrich, 165
Mitteldeutsche Privatbank, 50
Mixed ownership, 75, 76, 117
Mobilization, 116
Moratorium, 150, 189, 190, 193
Morocco, 55
Most Favored Nation Clause, 61, 62
Mozart, Wolfgang Amadeus, 8
Muller, Hermann, 196
Munich, 242
Municipalities, 30, 31, 46, 75, 77, 100, 122, 177, 188

Napoleon I, 10, 11, 25, 29
Narvik, xviii
Nationalbank für Deutschland, 50
National income, 219, 263
Nationalism, 10, 11, 14, 15, 61
Nationalization, 71, 75, 199-203, 233, 239, 240
National Socialism, xi, xii, 8, 16, 19, 77, 78, 82, 88, 92, 115, 119, 188, 222, 225, and Part V
Navy, 29, 60
Near East, 55, 58
NEP, 18
New York, 19, 54
Norddeutsche Bank, 49
   Wollkämmerei, 190

North Sea, 6
Norway, xvi-xviii
Nuremberg, 71

Oldenburg, 71
Optical industry, 177
Orientalische Eisenbahnen, 59

Pacific Ocean, 68
Palatinate, 7
Palestine, 35
Papen, Franz von, 222-225
Party program, 229-232
Paris Peace Treaties, 15
   Resolutions, 140
Passive resistance, 143, 144
Peace negotiations, 129
Persia, 59, 60
Poincaré, Raymond, 142, 150, 169
Poland, xviii, 6, 7, 14, 35, 40, 58
Population, 26, 38, 40
Portugal, 68
Post Office, 28-30, 76
Potash, 35, 83, 85, 86, 135, 201
Potatoes, 37, 113-115
Prague, 6
Price
   fixing, 202, 208, 210, 218, 244, 250, 258
   maximum, 112, 115, 119, 124
   political, 192, 194, 210
Prices, 82, 85, 86, 88, 102, 112, 152, 153, 159, 194, 195, 210, 245
Profit motive, 84
Promoters' boom, 25, 36
   Era, 72
Protectionism, 60-63, 65, 73, 78
Proudhon, Pierre Joseph, 46
Prosperity, 85, 176-185
   index, 171
Protestant Church, 183
Prussia, 7-16, 24, 27, 32, 36, 46, 60-62, 65, 67, 70-75, 117, 220-224, 230
Prussian Bank, 33, 77
Public works, 223, 239, 241, 242

292

Index

Purge, 234
Putsch, 134, 149, 221

Raiffeisen, 92
Railroads, 25-30, 36, 42, 56, 64, 65, 69, 71, 76, 136, 171, 174, 203, 206, 208
Rathenau, Emil, 43, 117, 236
  Walter, 43, 117-119, 150, 185
Rationalization, 176
Rationing, 113-115, 128
Raw materials, xv, 53, 69, 86, 97, 109, 111, 117-119, 123, 135, 251, 252
Reformation, 4, 6
Regulations, farm, 116, 123, 243, 246
  industries, 116, 117, 123, 198, 225, 277
Reich Debt Commission, 132
Reichsbank, 33, 45, 76, 97, 101, 104, 105, 107, 143, 155, 157, 166, 167, 174, 187-191, 206, 207, 249, 261, 272
Reich Coal Association, 201
  Council, 01
Reich Commissar for Prussia, 222
Reichsgericht, 223
Reichskreditgesellschaft, 205
Reichsland, 34
Reichsmark, 18, 33, 108
Reichsnährstand, 243
Reichsnotopfer, 148, 154
Reichspresident, 19
Reichstag, 5, 19, 79, 80, 98, 105, 129, 141, 221, 223-225, 230
Reichsverkehrsgesellschaft, 206
Rentenmark, 165, 168
  banknotes, 167
Reparations, 17, 18, 137-142, 169, 174, 179, 221, 222
Re-Privatising of Banks, 207
Resettlement, 184, 185
Revaluation, 160
Revolution, 15, 17, 95, 121, 128
  French, 9-11, 18

German, 1848, 11
Russian, 127-129
Rheinisch-Westphälische Elektrizitätswerke, 75, 158
Rhenish-Westphalian Coal Syndicate, 86
Riesser, J., 51
Rhine, 6, 8, 23, 241
Röhm, Ernst, 234
Rothschild, 46
Rubber, 69, 109
Ruhr, 18, 86, 128, 141, 144, 150, 163, 168, 169, 229
  Coal Syndicate, 201
Rumania, xviii, 14, 55, 58, 59, 109
Russia, xiv, xvi, 20, 40, 58, 64, 66, 138
Rye Mark, 165, 235

Saar, 17, 135
Sachlieferungen, 139, 141, 144
Sachwerte, 148, 157
Samoa, 68
Sanctions, 140, 142-144
Sarajevo, 14
Saxony, 7, 8, 28, 70, 72, 88
Scandinavia, xiv, xvi, xvii
Schaaffhausenscher Bankverein, 46, 47
Schacht, Hjalmar, 165, 188, 239, 272
Schleicher, Kurt von, 225
Schleichhandel, 108, 127
Schleswig-Holstein, 24
Schulze-Delitzsch, 92
Schulze-Gävernitz, G. von, 46
Schweitzer, J. von, 89
Serbia, 14, 96, 97
Shipbuilding, 49, 62
Shipping, 42, 56, 136, 138
Shop councils, 125, 199, 216, 218
  cells, 267
  leader, 267
Siemens, Werner von, 43
  Georg von, 236
Siemens-Schuckert A. G., 158

293

Index

Silesia, 8, 9, 17
  Upper, 128, 135, 136, 150
Silver, 32, 33
Smaller Germany, 24, 27
Socialist, 13, 16, 18, 75, 78, 79
Social-Democrats, 79, 80, 90, 98,
  121, 124, 127, 128, 148, 184, 199,
  221, 223, 230
  Independent, 121, 127
Social insurance, 16, 80, 82, 210,
  211, 270
Social Honor Courts, 268
Social reform, 77, 123
Soil Mark, 166
Sombart, Werner, 85
Spain, 4, 6
Spengler, Oswald, 16
"S.S." (Storm Troops), 234
Stabilization, 159, 162, 168
Stab in the Back, 125-128
Standstill Agreement, 192
State ownership, 70, 74, 77, 92
State socialism, 218
States, Federal, 3, 24, 32, 36, 74, 75,
  88, 100, 101, 112
"Statism," xi, 8-12, 16, 20, 118, 119,
  146, 198, 199, 239, 240, 272
Statistical Reich Bureau, 108
Steel, xviii, 34, 35, 42, 47, 85, 86,
  201
Sterling devaluation, 193
Stinnes, Hugo, 157, 159
Strasser, Gregor, 225, 243
Strength Through Joy, 269
Stresemann, Gustav, 143, 144, 159,
  165
Strikes, 122, 127, 129, 266
Sudetenland, 241, 262
Surtax, 31
Swabia, 7
Sweden, xvii, xviii, 7, 253
Switzerland, 5, 7, 15, 79, 80, 109,
  261
System, 219

Tariffs, 23, 37, 61-66, 85, 112

Tax certificates, 223
Taxes, 29, 30, 31, 98, 101, 104-106,
  146, 171, 263, 264, 269
Telegraph, 30, 76, 142
Tender, legal, 32, 100
Textiles, 26, 34, 61, 63, 65, 123,
  136, 177, 251
Thirty Years War, 4, 6, 8
Thomas, 34
Thyssen, August, 49
Trade
  Code, 82, 88
  illicit, 108, 127
  regulations, 27
  unions, 16, 78, 88, 90, 120, 122,
  124, 125, 216, 225
Transfer Committee, 180
Treasury, 31, 104
  bills, 45, 99, 100, 104, 105, 156
  certificates, 102-104
Trotzkyism, 235
Turkey, 55, 58, 59

Überwachungsstelle, 249
U-Boat War, 119
Ukrainia, 14, 109
Unemployment, 81, 122, 196, 198,
  230, 240, 241, 270
  relief, 122, 123, 217
Unification, 3, 23-25, 27, 60
United States of America, 25, 26,
  29, 32, 35, 39, 41, 44, 46, 52-58,
  63-68, 74, 83, 86, 96, 102, 110,
  126, 130, 134, 136, 173-177, 180,
  194, 206, 223, 253

Vaterländischer Hilfsdienst, 119,
  124, 125
Verein für Sozialpolitik, 78
Vereinigte Industrie A. G., 208
Vereinigte Stahlwerke, 159, 209
Versailles Treaty, xii, 15, 17, 35,
  135, 137, 235, 241
Vienna, 6
Volksgemeinschaft, 175, 192, 220

Index

Wages, 40, 123, 125, 161, 194, 197, 215, 258, 268, 270
  minimum, 124
War of 1870-1871, 3, 11, 62, 68, 99
War
  boom, 105, 123
  corporations, 100, 117, 119
  debt, 106
  economy, 19, 88, 96, 108
  financing, 96, 98, 100, 101, 103-106
  food administration, 111
  indemnity 1871, 35, 36, 56
  industries, 109, 120
  losses, 135
  pensions, 138
  profiteers, 105
  profits, 106, 118
  socialism, 108, 110, 119
Warburg, M. M. & Co., 54
Wechselordnung, 27
Wehrbeitrag, 31
Weimar Constitution, 19, 29, 30, 72, 74, 125, 146, 232
  period, 73, 77, 89, 92, 117, 119, 123, and Part IV

William I, 79
William II, 12, 17, 18, 80
Wilson, Woodrow, 137
Work Books, 270
Workers Committees, 124, 125
Work, Beauty of, 268
World War, 1914-1918, xvi, xvii, xix, 3, 13-17, 28, 30, 32, 37-39, 45-47, 51, 52, 56, 60, 66, 68, 69, 71, 75, 76, 85-88, 92, and Part III
World War, 1939, xi, xiv, xv, xvii, 3
Württemberg, 28, 71

Young, Owen D., 173
  Loan, 175, 189
  Plan, 172-175, 179, 188, 231
Yugoslavia, 14

Zanzibar, 67
Zellwolle, 252
Zinc, 135
Zürich, 59, 79
Zollverein, 24, 25, 27, 29, 31, 61, 62, 67

295